Praise for –

God's Powerful Vision for Your Life: The BIG Idea

"Greg's insights are unique and thought-provoking. This is a deep and encouraging dive into your faith and how God can use you to influence others. You will be a better leader after reading this book."

- Lilya Wagner, Ph.D., Director, Philanthropic Service for Institutions; Adjunct Faculty Member, Lilly Family School of Philanthropy

---

"Nehemiah had never been recognized as a great figure in biblical history until Greg Long highlighted his amazing accomplishment in rebuilding the wall around Jerusalem and powerfully applied this miracle for leaders today."

- Patrick Hurley, Emmy award winning producer and writer

"Greg's narrative of Nehemiah, and his story, brought whole new meaning and importance to me to this ancient story. You'll think differently about your leadership after reading this book."

- Tom Pound, Senior Pastor, Spring Hills Church, Granville, Ohio

---

"Greg's book is for anyone who is a leader and includes important topics such as: vision, communication, integrity, staying true and authentic, developing others, focus, dealing with naysayers, and answering a "calling." Insightful and practical. From the Old Testament, but relevant for today's world."

- Nancy Short, Servant Leadership Facilitator and Executive Director, Ransburg YMCA, Indianapolis, Indiana

---

"This is a book about leadership, about big ideas. It's a book that grapples with the real issues of how to lead, engage, and motivate others in a working environment too often filled with distractors, disruptors, and detractors. It's a book about overcoming the odds, tenacity, trust, and faithfulness. The book is well written, extremely practical, sometimes entertaining, and just when you might least expect it both inspiring and convicting. Add it to your reading list, you just might be motivated to pursue your big idea!"

- Gerald H. Twombly, President and Founder, 100 Nations Campaign, LTD

"I continuously seek books that challenge my leadership to be consistent with my values and faith. "God's Powerful Vision for Your Life: The Big Idea" does just that. In this book, as you journey with Nehemiah as he seeks to complete the vision God planted in his heart, be prepared to reflect on the things that God is equipping you to do through your own leadership. This book is a refreshing change from the "step by step how to" approach found in other books. It will challenge you to reflect deeply on your motives, needs and desire to serve God in your leadership roles."

- Kim Ramsey-White, Ph.D., Servant Leadership Expert & Trainer and Undergraduate Program Director, Georgia State University School of Public Health

----

Think you've "heard it all" when it comes to the Book of Nehemiah? Perish the thought. Greg delivers an affable, inspiring, and extremely practical read that challenges you and I to reconsider what God wants accomplished and how to lead so those Big Ideas become reality. You'll find yourself compelled to take notes and mark pages as you come across invaluable insights, so grab a pen and start reading!

Randy Beaverson, Director, Asia-Pacific region, Youth for Christ International

----

"The Big Idea is a book about a big vision to live a big life because of a big God. Don't get caught up in small thinking, small planning, small goals, small vision, and small living. God created you for much more. Greg Long offers you a timely biblical reminder in these pages. Take and read."

- Dan DeWitt (PhD, The Southern Baptist Theological Seminary) is associate professor of applied theology and apologetics and the director the Center for Biblical Apologetics and Public Christianity at Cedarville University. He is the author of *Jesus or Nothing* (Crossway, 2014) and *Christ or Chaos* (Crossway, 2016). He posts regularly on his

----

From Amazon:

Geoff U. *4.0 out of 5 stars*

Clear guidance to lead you to fulfill dreams by team building. Long elucidates leadership dynamics that demand consideration. He takes the classic narrative of Nehemiah to inspire his readers to do great things while building healthy functional teams.

Joe P. *5.0 out of 5 stars*

WOW! This book is destined for greatness. It had me hooked by the third chapter and stimulated my interest throughout. I loved how the author, Greg Long, wrapped things together. This is a must read!

Amazon Customer, Transformed *5.0 out of 5 stars*

Good read, whether you have faith or not. Interesting, contemporary topic of Nehemiah. He was an important figure in the Old Testament. Nehemiah and how he approaches his project and all the related problems & opportunities is not only interesting but completely applicable to what we face today. Good read, whether you have faith or not.

James V. *5.0 out of 5 stars*

Much Needed Message. What I love about this book is that it takes spiritual and moral principles and applies them not only to leadership but life. Loved it.

God's Powerful Vision for Your Life

God's Powerful Vision for Your Life:

The BIG Idea

Gregory Long, M.A.

ISBN 978-0-9976118-0-9

God's Powerful Vision for Your Life:
The BIG Idea

© 2017 by Gregory Long, M.A.
Published by Gregory Long Leadership
4th Printing, March 2021

ISBN 978-0-9976118-0-9

Cover Art: Sara DeVere (www.deverecreative.com)

ACKNOWLEDGEMENTS

MANY thanks for the people who helped me complete this BIG Idea.

Elaine, Sara & Ryan – too many ways to list.

Ari – for smiles, laughs and sweet reminders of Greg.

Steve & Marla, Julie & John – for doing life with us for so many years.

Tom L., Nory, Karen & Larry, Jeff, Tom P. – for praying weekly for me & for this book over the life of the project.

For Craig – who invested time and truly changed the path of my life.

Pat – for his invaluable help as writer coach and editor.

Dick P. – who I haven't talked with in 40 years, but whose teaching series on Nehemiah started this BIG Idea.

Much love and appreciation,
Greg

God's Powerful Vision for Your Life

CONTENTS

PROLOGUE

The BIG Idea.

What is it?

It's an idea that will not let go of you, because the God of the Universe planted it in your heart, mind and soul. It is a vision from Him to do something about something.

It is a BIG Idea that you cannot ignore, avoid or escape. And, you shouldn't because Almighty God put it there.

There have been hundreds of BIG Ideas in the Bible. They were fought on the battlegrounds of faith, tears, trust and courage in the power of the Holy Spirit.

Now, it is your turn.

This book is for leaders. It is for people who dream BIG, and who want to live BIG. For people with a BIG Idea!

I believe everyone has a BIG Idea in them. Something they feel deeply about, a problem in society that they see or feel.

You may first dismiss the BIG Idea, thinking it's crazy, far-fetched, or unattainable.

You may try to ignore it, but it's seared in your heart. You may try to escape it, because you don't think you have the talent, education or skill to pull it off.

But, you know that you are the person God wants to anoint in pursuing this BIG Idea. You feel it deep in your bones.

It will not go away. It will never go away. And, you will not be satisfied until you do something about it.

You will need to rally others to help you until you complete the vision God gave you.

But, complete it you must. This is not negotiable. You are dealing with God's powerful vision for *your* life.

Obey Him.

You will make a positive change in the lives of people. They will be transformed. That is called *servant leadership*, my friend.

You will be transformed, too. You will see how the BIG Idea stirring in your soul can propel you into being a leader.

God did not put you on this earth to follow – but to step out in faith and lead.

> **Now faith is the assurance of things hoped for, the conviction of things not seen. For by it the men of old gained approval. Hebrews 11:1-2**

I have focused on the Book of Nehemiah to detail The BIG Idea and how God makes it a reality.

Nehemiah was not a leader; he was just a faithful servant. He had no personal stake in rebuilding that wall. In fact, he had never even been to Jerusalem.

That made no difference to God.

He chose Nehemiah for the task to accomplish the miraculous feat. He put The BIG Idea into the humble cupbearer's heart and what happened after that was more than amazing.

Our world needs more Nehemiahs. I pray that God uses this book to plant a BIG Idea in you. And, that you run with that Idea and change lives.

This is not only my tribute to one of the greatest leaders who ever lived, it is a practical guide for any leader today on how to plan and succeed with passion.

I hope you enjoy it. I also pray that God uses the story of Nehemiah to help you launch the <u>BIG Idea</u> He's planted in you.

Gregory Long

DEDICATION

To our son Greg, who joined Jesus way too early. He lived out BIG Ideas and left an example and legacy for dozens of his peers and their parents.

He would have been side-by-side with Nehemiah, immersed in the tough work of wall building – and the significant work of people building.

I pray his BIG Ideas continue on in me, and in you.

CHAPTER 1
800 MILES
Nehemiah 1:1-11

Congratulations!

You are a Leader.

You've been appointed to a new position. You've been elected to a new team or committee.

Or, you've been hired to a new job, and you're the top dog, the Chief Executive Officer (CEO), the Prez, the big Kahuna, Numero Uno. Excitement awaits you. Fresh challenges. New adventures.

A chance for you to make your mark in an agency or field or industry.

An opportunity to make a positive difference in the lives of people. You are going to rewrite history.

And, you are scared witless.

You've never been a leader before, at least not in this sense. Or, not at this level.

With the adventure, challenge and excitement, you're trembling inside, like the time you stepped onto your first roller coaster ride. Or, your first kiss, which is a roller coaster ride with *lips!*

Or, your first road trip with friends. There's excitement and terror pulsing through your veins all at the same time.

Condolences

You're the leader.

You've been chosen to revive a dying organization. Or, you were in the wrong place at the wrong time. You missed the meeting, and in your absence, someone nominated you to be *in charge*.

You weren't even there to defend yourself.

Your new job wasn't at all what they described in the job interview. You've been *volun-told* for a new project – one that nobody else wanted.

My condolences.

This isn't what you signed up for. This was part of the fine print that no one pointed out. It's like the feeling after your minor first car wreck. You feel fine at first and then your legs tremble uncontrollably. You're light-headed. You feel a little sick to your stomach.

Understandable. And...unavoidable.

Since you are now a leader, voluntarily or involuntarily, I have someone for you to meet. Whether it's a role you chased, because you were excited and clueless, or you were trapped like a rat on a sinking ship, pay attention here.

My associate will clear a path for you in your leadership position.

This heroic historical figure will be able to help you make sense of leadership and your role as a leader. He will give *you* ideas, tips, and approaches to enhance your leadership no matter who you are, where you are, or the group you are leading.

His name is Nehemiah.

He lived and led 2,500 years ago. His confidence, philosophy, methods and ultimate success changed the course of history, including mine. He was a leader with passion, ingenuity and boldness.

You can be, too. Let's read a bit from his biography.

Nehemiah 1:1-11

> **The words of Nehemiah son of Hakaliah:**
>
> **In the month of Kislev in the twentieth year, while I was in the citadel of Susa, Hanani, one of my brothers, came from Judah with some other men, and questioned them about the Jewish remnant that had survived the exile, and also about Jerusalem.**

They said to me, "Those who survived the exile and are back in the province are in great trouble and disgrace. The wall of Jerusalem is broken down, and its gates have been burned with fire."

When I heard these things, I sat down and wept. For some days, I mourned and fasted and prayed before the God of heaven.

Then I said: "Lord, the God of heaven, the great and awesome God, who keeps His covenant of love with those who love Him and keep His commandments, let Your ear be attentive and Your eyes open to hear the prayer Your servant is praying before You day and night for Your servants, the people of Israel. I confess the sins we Israelites, including myself and my father's family, have committed against You. We have acted very wickedly toward You. We have not obeyed the commands, decrees and laws You gave Your servant Moses.

Remember the instruction You gave your servant Moses, saying, 'If you are unfaithful, I will scatter you among the nations, but if you return to Me and obey My commands, then even if your exiled people are at the farthest horizon, I will gather them from there and bring them to the place I have chosen as a dwelling for my Name.'

They are Your servants and Your people, whom You redeemed by Your great strength and Your mighty hand. Lord, let Your ear be attentive to the prayer of this Your servant and to the prayer of Your servants who delight in revering Your name. Give Your servant success today by granting him favor in the presence of this man."

I was cupbearer to the king.

Really? A waiter? Someone who worked in the king's kitchen?

Doesn't sound like a leader to you?

Just wait.

Let's look at the situation in which Nehemiah found himself.

Let's begin by checking out the distances between these locations in terms of mileage:

Columbus, Ohio to Orlando
Denver to Phoenix
Montreal to Charlotte
Naples, Italy to Paris, France

800 miles

A quick trip by today's air travel standards. Longer and perhaps more tedious if you drive. An ordeal if you had to walk that distance.

What gets you amped up about traveling 800 miles?

Vacation?
Family reunions?
Family funeral?
An excellent meal?
A new job or career opportunity?

What excites you enough to travel 800 miles?

When I was a boy, my family traveled each summer from our home in central Indiana to Northern Wisconsin. The distance of our journey was 650 miles.

We would jam our family of four into our Ford station wagon, along with all our suitcases, rods and reels, and snack food for the drive. Then, we'd head north to my grandparent's house a short distance away.

Two hours. I was already bored.

After a late breakfast, we'd all pack into the car again, this time with my grandmother and grandfather. We'd head toward Chicago, where my Aunt Marge and Uncle Jack lived.

More time in the car.

More sitting.

Not good for a boy eight years old. I recall one year, we left the trusty station wagon in the garage and took my dad's new luxury sedan. I had to sit on Grandma's lap, wedged in the back seat, leaning sideways, against the side door, the handle stabbing my back and the window creasing my shoulder.

I felt like I was crammed inside a can of tuna.

After a very short period of time my leg started to cramp up. I asked the question every young boy demands on a family road trip, *Are we there yet?!*

My Dad gritted his teeth and gripped the steering wheel.

I recall the ride to the rented lake cottage in Wisconsin being filled with road constructions, National Guard convoys and bumper-to-bumper traffic jams. To intensify the agony, Dad turned off the air conditioning so the car wouldn't overheat.

With the windows down, we were treated to the humid, sticky July heat that hung on our bodies like a sweaty stalker ignoring a heat-seeking restraining order.

The aroma…no…stench of diesel fumes from the long-haul trucks filled our noses. Nothing about the trip itself was a good memory for me. It was a mobile toxic waste dump through the Gobi Desert, only with humidity.

However, once we arrived at the cabin, all the frustration and misery of our journey from Hades disappeared. The gentle breeze in the birch trees, the comforting sound of the thumping waves against the docked boats and the distant call of a Loon magically erased the memory of the 650 mile ordeal, seemingly in an instant.

What horrible car ride?

There is nowhere on the face of the planet where I feel closer to God than on a lake in the North Woods. I know that God is always close to me. But in the wondrous calm and stillness of the trees, water and wildlife, I have a deeper appreciation of His creation and His love for me.

Despite the rigorous, brutal journey in my eight year-old mind, I'd go back every time.

The end result was always worth the journey.

Nehemiah was so motivated about his project that he traveled 800 miles. He did this without any modern conveniences, no air-conditioning, no convenience store snacks, no smooth roads, and probably a lot of it on foot.

He traveled 800 miles to do what he believed he was supposed to do. Something he couldn't shake, ignore or avoid.

800 miles to rebuild a wall around Jerusalem.

800 miles to rebuild a people.

800 miles to lead an effort that God had uniquely called him to do.

It was his time to be a leader to those who desperately needed one.

Nehemiah, as far as we know, was never a leader before this time. He was new to this position.

Perhaps, just like you.

His story of success is worth your time to read and imitate. The following pages will change your life as a leader.

That is my promise to you.

Now, for the back story…

God's Chosen People, the Israelites, were once a mighty force in the ancient world. The Old Testament and other literature are filled with examples of how God blessed His people when they were obedient and followed His principles and commandments.

There were also very unpleasant consequences when they did not obey God. As a result of their disobedience, there were tortuous examples of God's people being beaten, captured, and murdered by their enemies.

Whether you believe the literal words in the Old Testament or not, the historical fact of the Jewish people and their roller coaster of captivity is well documented.

Nehemiah's story as a new leader opened in what is now the modern-day city of Shush, near the far western border of Iran. This is about 450 years before the birth of Jesus and the Roman Empire. Most scholars believe Nehemiah is one of the last books written of the Old Testament.

Approximately 160 years before, the Israelites were taken over and captured by the Babylonians. Remember Nebuchadnezzar, the king of the Babylonians, that guy Daniel, the lion's den, and the three guys in a fiery furnace that lived to tell about it?

The Babylonians were, in turn, conquered by the Persians.

Each time a new king was victorious, God's Chosen People, the Israelites, were scattered throughout the new kingdom, serving as slaves and laborers for that empire.

This is probably how Nehemiah's family ended up in Susa. Nehemiah's forerunners had likely been taken captive and relocated from Israel and Jerusalem to the Persian capital – 800 miles away.

There's no clear record that Nehemiah had ever lived in Jerusalem. In fact, it's highly likely that Nehemiah had never even *visited* Jerusalem, the city of his ancestors.

But, that did not dampen his passion for God's holy city.

When Nehemiah heard from a group of travelers that Jerusalem was completely destroyed, he was moved to save it. The city where God's People were to live, work, and worship was completely run-down and unlivable.

The biblical narrative confirmed that the **walls were broken down and the gates were burned by fire (v. 3).**

How would you feel if you learned that your family's home, your high school or home town was destroyed by an earthquake, tornado, tsunami or in this case, by a violent act of terrorism?

You've no doubt seen the photos and news clips of the aftermath of a hurricane. I believe Jerusalem was in the same condition. Thousands stepped up to help the communities destroyed by the hurricanes.

Nehemiah found himself in this heart-wrenching situation. His spirit was as crushed and shattered as the broken and crumbled walls of Jerusalem.

And most significantly, he had never been there!

He'd never experienced the vitality of the city market. He'd never worshiped in the Temple that King David founded and King Solomon built.

It would be like me constantly hearing about the joy and beauty of the North Woods from my family, but never experiencing it for myself.

We read that after hearing of the state of Jerusalem, that Nehemiah, **...sat down and wept. For some days, I mourned and fasted and prayed before the God of heaven. (1:4).**

By the way, if you look closely at the *days* that Nehemiah fasted and prayed, it was actually four *months!*

The month Kislev (Neh. 1:1) runs from approximately the middle of November to the middle of December in our current calendar. The month Nisan (Neh. 2:1) correlates with the middle of March to mid-April.

So, Nehemiah's idea percolated and simmered for four months while he fasted and prayed.

Some days, huh?

Talk about an understatement!

Nehemiah was so moved that he was unable to eat...really?

What is so important in your life that you cannot eat because it's not going well?

Hand me just about anything, Oreos, a burger, pizza with extra cheese...I'm IN!

In your professional life, when was the last time your board, trustees or elders were so distraught over a situation in your organization that they couldn't eat?

When was the last time YOU were so bent out of shape that you couldn't eat?

What was so terrible that it made you sick?

I mean, this is **serious** folks.

I see many people in positions of influence, leadership and power, overseeing people and programs that they could easily walk away from. They were unemployed and somehow landed a job in an organization with a cause they couldn't embrace.

Don't get me wrong; a job is important. I've been unemployed and under-employed, and personal income is a necessity. The point here is that a person in leadership had better be *driven, motivated and amped up* by the organization's cause.

Who wants to lead a group of people in a cause they don't care about?

So, let's reverse this concept and ask some questions:

What makes you excited?
What problems challenge you to solve them?
What cause, mission or need would make you travel 800 miles to tackle it?

I bet you have a Big Idea inside you. It's a feeling or insight that will not go away. You can't ignore it. You can't avoid it. You cannot escape it.

Here are some possibilities…do any of these strike a passionate chord in you?

Bolstering and helping the homeless.

Caring for the aging and physically challenged.

Furnishing needed items for international immigrants and refugees.

Leading people in joyous and inspired singing at a church.

Teaching others how to teach.

Equipping people with the financial skills to earn, save and spend effectively.

Supporting women with an unexpected pregnancy.

Assisting people displaced and traumatized by a natural disaster.

Restoring green space for community recreation.

Rehabbing homes and improving neighborhoods.

Comforting people who are at the end of their life.

Helping young couples be better parents to their kids.

Helping single moms and dads manage their children, job and life.

Building a wall around Jerusalem.

On a personal level, as a leader, what's your mission? What gets your heart beating fast? What problems haunt you? What problems beg you to help find a solution? What solution causes you to smile wide in the car when you are all by yourself? What would cause you to fast and pray for four months?

I think I know what drove Nehemiah.

He knew the history of God's people and God's promises. He knew his people were devastated in Jerusalem. He knew that what was happening to the Israelites needed the grace of God to heal and restore them.

Nehemiah knew God's promises.

In **Nehemiah 1:5-11**, he begs God, agreeing that the Israelites were in slavery because they had not obeyed Him. Nehemiah understood the consequences that would happen when the Israelites did not follow God.

The wall around their beloved city had been devastated.

Like the Apostle Paul's protégé in 2 Timothy 1:5, it is likely that Nehemiah had a God-fearing and obedient family member.

Young Timothy had a devout grandmother who taught him the promises and principles of Scripture. It appears that the same family situation and history was present in Nehemiah's life.

Someone in his life had taught him God's law and His promises.

Someone had instilled in him the need to rebuild that wall.

Without that physical protection, the Israelites were in serious danger of being overthrown by other countries as a result of their disregard and disobedience towards the Almighty God.

Sin, going against God's wishes and guidance, had put them in this precarious position. Nehemiah's heart for God and his prayer for the blessing to rebuild the wall were the only hope the Israelites had to survive in the future.

Two practical thoughts here for us:

1. Your faith drives how you lead. Your values, convictions and choices should be based on a faith in what is good and right. That faith should also be based on a Higher Power. My moral compass is based on the God of the Bible and the historical person of Jesus Christ. Your moral compass might be linked to something else.

2. Hang on to that value and belief that guides you. Follow it in your everyday life and as the foundation for all your decisions. And, read on to see how Nehemiah, someone who believes in God, can lead and get results.

Because of my faith in God and His Son Jesus, I have survived a devastating death in my family and several personal crises. My trust in Him has enabled me to experience personally powerful, life-transforming events.

Whatever has happened to me, both good and bad, I have never let go of my faith. My God of grace has gently seen me through every heartbreak and headache.

I encourage you to always stand by your faith and be dead-set and driven by your mission.

Nehemiah didn't sway from his God or his mission. He is a worthy example for us to follow.

We're just getting started!

CHAPTER 2
HEY, WHAT'S ~~THE~~ YOUR BIG IDEA?
Nehemiah 2:1-9

Make no little plans. They have no magic to stir men's blood and probably will not themselves be realized. - Daniel Burnham

Big Ideas

Maybe you have never heard of Daniel Burnham. I heard this quote many years ago and have used it in countless presentations and meetings for a long time before actually paying attention to the man who said it.

Burnham was a Chicago-based architect who lived in the late 1800s and into the early 20th Century. He was one of the most noted building designers of his day.

He was instrumental in helping create the master plans for cities like Chicago, Illinois and Manila, Philippines. One of his most-recognized works is Union Station in Washington, DC.

Burnham had Big Ideas!

He could *see* a city or a building in his mind's eye before it was ever plotted on a blueprint. He saw entire cities, skyscrapers, city parks and green spaces.

He could see possibilities - and then go out and *create* them. He had Big Ideas and stirred men's blood to go and build them. To this day, many of us still admire and respect his work.

One of my trips to Washington, D.C. stands out and involves the iconic Union Station. Union Station is the historic train depot for the U.S. capital. All trains and the Metro subway system link to this transportation landmark.

It was early morning. I had flown into Baltimore before sunrise, jumped on an Amtrak train and found myself coming out of Union Station at daybreak.

I walked out the archways and across the drive and headed to the taxi stand.

As I waited for my cab, an echoing chorus of "Amazing Grace" carried across the sky. I was mesmerized. I could hear it, but I couldn't figure out where the music was coming from. Even as the taxi was pulling up to meet me I still couldn't locate the source of the enchanting tune.

Then, my eye caught a bright flash off to my right. I turned and saw a lone trumpet player standing under an archway, playing this powerful inspirational hymn.

He was a street performer standing proudly in the sunlight as it reflected off the brass bell of his horn. He was using the arches of Union Station to propel his music across the entire parking area.

The music resonated off the limestone arches and walls as it magically amplified for everyone on the sidewalk to hear – and enjoy.

I waved the taxi driver past. Instead of boarding my cab I needed to hear more. I stepped out of the taxi waiting line, lugging my briefcase back across the roadway. I dropped a couple of bucks into the musician's open trumpet case, smiled and thanked the performer as he continued to play.

My entire day was brightened in that *magical* moment.

Nearly 100 years after Burnham designed Union Station, his creation still *stirred men's souls*.

No little plans.

Big Ideas.

There are moments, events and challenges that define our greatness.
The exquisite line that determines the everyday from the excellent.
The accomplishment that not only moves the world around us, but changes it for the better.

We all need to heed the call to pursue greatness. We were never created to live a life of quiet desperation as Henry David Thoreau called it. We don't always have to trudge along the ground. Sometimes, we need to reach for the stars.

How does a leader respond to a Big Idea?

Let Nehemiah show us the way.

Nehemiah 2:1-9

In the month of Nisan in the twentieth year of King Artaxerxes, when wine was brought for him, I took the wine and gave it to the king. I had not been sad in his presence before, so the king asked me, "Why does your face look so sad when you are not ill? This can be nothing but sadness of heart."

I was very much afraid, but I said to the king, "May the king live forever! Why should my face not look sad when the city where my ancestors are buried lies in ruins, and its gates have been destroyed by fire?"

The king said to me, "What is it you want?" Then I prayed to the God of heaven, and I answered the king, "If it pleases the king and if your servant has found favor in his sight, let him send me to the city in Judah where my ancestors are buried so that I can rebuild it."

Then the king, with the queen sitting beside him, asked me, "How long will your journey take, and when will you get back?" It pleased the king to send me; so I set a time.

I also said to him, "If it pleases the king, may I have letters to the governors of Trans-Euphrates, so that they will provide me safe-conduct until I arrive in Judah? And may I have a letter to Asaph, keeper of the royal park, so he will give me timber to make beams for the gates of the citadel by the temple and for the city wall and for the residence I will occupy?" And because the gracious hand of my God was on me, the king granted my requests. So I went to the governors of Trans-Euphrates and gave them the king's letters. The king had also sent army officers and cavalry with me.

Any Big Idea, whether it be a major project or a significant accomplishment rarely happens alone. There's always a team involved.

At Daniel Burnham's death, he was the leader of the largest architectural firm on earth and, not coincidentally, Burnham had a *team*. He knew the drill.

It was never just him; it was always *we!*

That's how the relationship between leaders and their Big Ideas works.

As we continue reading through Nehemiah, we will see this is true in the rebuilding of the wall of Jerusalem as well.

If you are a leader, then your leadership needs to be about *relationships*. People need to follow you and help you get your Big Ideas accomplished.

Nehemiah was no exception.

In this case, it's interesting to realize Nehemiah, was in fact, a follower.

He was not the leader of Persia. He was simply a respected worker in the king's court. God honored his relationship with the king of Persia and as a result, many doors were opened that allowed Nehemiah to launch and fulfill the Big Idea that was on his heart.

There are several examples in the Bible in which the person God used to fulfill His promise or complete the Big Idea, wasn't always the leader.

When they were kings of Israel, both Saul and David won battles and displayed (at times) the majesty of God's kingdom by the way they followed God.

This was also true of Daniel, Esther, and Joseph and the Big Ideas that God used in their lives, as well.

All these individuals had very *different* circumstances, and each of these *second-in-command* individuals gained and earned the respect and regard of the leader in power.

In God's supreme plan for him, Nehemiah developed a relationship with King Artaxerxes, built on trust and respect. He was the cupbearer to the king. The ruler's very life is dependent on whether or not the cupbearer is truthful, trustworthy and loyal. This is not merely a key position in the palace. It is one that may determine life or death.

In movies and literature, we see the example of someone tasting food and drink for a king to protect him from being poisoned by his enemies. This was no small task and never one to be taken lightly.

I am speculating a bit on how this practice happened in those days.

Did Nehemiah eat food in front of the king - and then if he didn't pass out, or die within a half an hour - was the food then judged safe to be eaten by the king?

Whatever the process that was used, King Artaxerxes clearly believed he could trust Nehemiah with his very life.

Despite being a Jew and probably a common laborer in the king's court, Nehemiah earned the king's respect, trust and admiration.

Because he had won over the king's admiration, Nehemiah now had an opportunity to use this personal relationship to help him with his Big Idea.

After four months of praying, fasting and planning how he could get to Jerusalem to help rebuild the wall, Nehemiah had a chance to bring up his Big Idea with the king of Persia.

At some point in this process, Artaxerxes realized a change in Nehemiah's attitude and demeanor.

Perhaps Nehemiah wasn't as talkative as usual in the presence of the king. Maybe Nehemiah had more of a solemn look on his face.

Whatever the external signals given by Nehemiah, the king *noticed*. Here was Nehemiah's chance to make his Big Idea his Big Dream come true.

Anyone can come up with a creative notion, but most people never see it realized. This Big Idea had the potential to change history. The Great Wall of Jerusalem would ensure the safety and survival of the Israelites forever.

What if Nehemiah never shared his Big Idea?

This timely interaction between Nehemiah and Artaxerxes was not a coincidence. It was a carefully orchestrated event laid down by a Sovereign Planner at the foundation of the world. God had purposed for this wall to be rebuilt and He called Nehemiah to accomplish it.

This was eternally deliberate.

That is why God's Big Ideas, when they are set before us, will never fail. But, we have to immerse ourselves in His Spirit and be obedient and faithful to follow Him to that success.

If you're a Jesus follower, then I assure you this was a God-ordained moment paving the way for Nehemiah to ask for a big favor in order to pursue his Big Idea of solving a big problem.

In **Nehemiah 2:4**, the king directly asked what Nehemiah wants and Nehemiah quickly prayed. Remember, he had been praying for four months. This wasn't the first time he'd taken this Big Idea before God.

But, this may have been the first time he had a chance to communicate his Big Idea to anyone other than himself. I suspect this prayer before the king lasted about 1 ½ seconds, as in,

God, Help!

Nehemiah essentially asked for permission to take a leave of absence from his job as cupbearer, to go to a city that he had never visited, to rebuild the wall that he had never seen.

Minor details for one of the greatest miracles in history.

When was the last time you had to ask a favor of your boss? Or your board? Or your spouse?

The possibility that King Artaxerxes would even consider Nehemiah's request was in direct proportion to the *relationship* Nehemiah had with the king.
Their connection to each other had been no accident.

As previously noted, I believe God set it up.

Keep remembering that. It will speak to your heart when it comes time for you to propose your Big Idea. It's God's Big Idea; He wants you to succeed and accomplish it.

> **Now faith is confidence in what we hope for and assurance about what we do not see. (Hebrews 11:1)**

Nehemiah exercised His trust in an Almighty God, as well as his self-respect and his spiritual boldness to lay out his idea. The king respected the servant enough to hear him out.

The king's heart was divinely stirred.

Do you respect yourself enough to stick to an idea that you believe in?

Or, do you water down your plans and ideas, fearing that your listeners will laugh, mock or discard it?

Are you nervous to share Big Plans? Do *your* plans stir the soul?

There is only one way to find out the answer.

Go to your Creator and prayerfully ask Him to not only give you that Big Idea but to empower it to the end.

We have all been in meetings, conferences or situations in which someone is only participating to push his or her idea, agenda, product or service. He is self–serving and myopic and not interested in anyone's welfare but his *own*.

It will take God's grace, wisdom and courage to ensure these individuals - individuals with their own idea and agenda - do not derail your Big Idea.

Nehemiah will demonstrate these assets as we watch him deal with others who have a selfish agenda.

The king of Persia was the most powerful person on the face of the planet. King Artaxerxes had prestige, force, riches, control and authority. It was his army that defeated the Babylonians, who had defeated the Israelites.

Now a trusted, but common servant was asking for a leave of absence to travel 800 miles to rebuild the walls of a capital city.

Artaxerxes had everything to lose in this scenario. If he gives Nehemiah permission, he loses a trusted and valued servant.

AND, if Nehemiah was *successful* during his leave of absence and rebuilds the wall of Jerusalem, the Israelites would become a powerful nation again and threaten King Artaxerxes' kingdom and authority.

There is no logical, earthly reason for King Artaxerxes to grant Nehemiah's request, but he *did*.

He agreed and gave permission for Nehemiah to go to Jerusalem.

Nehemiah also asks for permission to obtain timber from the king's forest along the way. In addition, the king provides an armed guard for Nehemiah's trip to Jerusalem.

This is of God, there is no way any of this makes any human sense.

What God originates, He orchestrates. – Andy Stanley

Nehemiah's trust in God and his respectful relationship with the king launches his Big Idea to travel to rebuild the city.

As far as we can tell here, Nehemiah wasn't a city planner. He didn't have a graduate degree in civil engineering. We're not sure Nehemiah could even swing a hammer!

Nehemiah has none of the qualifications that Daniel Burnham, a professional architect, possessed.

However, Nehemiah's relationship with Artaxerxes, and his understanding of God's promises, drove his obedience to do what God called him to do.

Rebuild the wall!

God's moment in time, coupled with an obedient, respect-filled individual who knew God's purpose, caused the most powerful ruler on earth to agree to a project that could bring down his own empire.

Wow.

CHAPTER 3
GETTING THE WORD OUT
Nehemiah 2:11-20

If your actions inspire others to dream more, learn more, do more and become more, you are a leader. - John Quincy Adams

In this day and age, when a president, prime minister, ambassador or any other high official arrives in a different county, the first order of business is usually a press conference.

There are smiles all around, photo ops, handshakes, an exchange of gifts, and carefully crafted statements announcing how the discussions will dramatically affect the lives of people from both countries.

If you are a sports or entertainment celebrity, you will craft a photogenic exit from a limousine, making sure the journalists and paparazzi have a perfect shot of you, ensuring maximum exposure of your beauty and notoriety.

Not Nehemiah.

Nehemiah 2:11-20

> **I went to Jerusalem, and after staying there three days, I set out during the night with a few others. I had not told anyone what my God had put in my heart to do for Jerusalem. There were no mounts with me except the one I was riding on.**

> **By night, I went out through the Valley Gate toward the Jackal Well and the Dung Gate, examining the walls of Jerusalem, which had been broken down, and its gates, which had been destroyed by fire. Then I moved on toward the Fountain Gate and the King's Pool, but there was not enough room for my mount to get through; so I went up the valley by night, examining the wall.**

Finally, I turned back and reentered through the Valley Gate. The officials did not know where I had gone or what I was doing, because as yet I had said nothing to the Jews or the priests or nobles or officials or any others who would be doing the work.

Nehemiah had just traveled 800 miles, which was a three-month journey back in his day, and finally arrived in Jerusalem.

The city had been virtually destroyed. Many of the Israelites who resided there were actually living, not in the broken down city, but in the provinces and plains surrounding it.

It was heartbreaking for them.

Since Nehemiah had not even been to Jerusalem, (his ancestors had been captured by invading armies generations ago) he didn't even know the *layout* of the city.

Yet, here he was, pursing the vision that God had rooted and grown in his heart.

At the same time Nehemiah entered the gates of Jerusalem, it was understood that a representative of the King of Persia was in town. It is significant to note that Nehemiah had an entourage alongside him, too. Remember, the king's guard, workers with timbers, advisors, and no doubt others, had made the trip with Nehemiah.

Nehemiah had not arrived unnoticed. There were whispers all over the surrounding provinces, proclaiming his trip to Jerusalem.

Today, there would be press leaks, social media blitzes and buzz on the street trumpeting, *This is the man who will rebuild our wall!*

Nope, that is NOT how it went down.

For three days, Nehemiah just hung out and walked around the wall, making mental notes. I am speculating here. The story doesn't really detail his activities for those three days. But, he kept a low profile, under the radar to anyone in or near the city.

There was no indication of state dinners and photo ops. No celebrity sightings. No paparazzi.

After three days, under the cover of night, Nehemiah and a handful of men scouted the city walls in detail. He wanted to see for himself how bad the situation really was, and the challenge before him.

It was bad. Recall the worst hurricane you've ever seen or heard about. It was this bad.

The walls were actually mounds of rubble. Openings that used to hold strong wooden gates, securing the city, were now in ruins. Nehemiah probably couldn't even tell where the original city boundaries were supposed be.

At one point in his reconnaissance, Nehemiah couldn't even walk all the way around the city due to the wreckage, broken rock and debris.

He had to turn back.

The work in front of him was a disaster beyond his imagination.

Finally, Nehemiah had his press conference. He called together many of the people still living in Jerusalem and delivered his mission statement.

Nehemiah 2:17-18

> **Then I said to them, "You see the trouble we are in: Jerusalem lies in ruins, and its gates have been burned with fire. Come, let us rebuild the wall of Jerusalem, and we will no longer be in disgrace." I also told them about the gracious hand of my God on me and what the king had said to me.**
>
> **The residents shouted, "Let us start rebuilding." So they began this good work.**

Passion is good.

So they got to work.

Leaders, Information & Innovation

Slip on a pair of time-traveling sandals. Imagine you are living in Nehemiah's day. You're an Israelite living in or near Jerusalem. A few days ago, a huge caravan of guards, servants, and an ambassador for the King of Persia arrived in your city.

What's going on here?

Rumors and confusion run rampant. There is speculation, skepticism and supposition on everyone's lips.

No one could make any sense of it.

If you were living in that day what conclusion would you come to?

For the record, you wouldn't be receiving any clues from the man who came to rebuild your wall.

It's not clear why Nehemiah did not immediately announce his purpose to the residents of Jerusalem. Maybe he was tired after traveling for three months. His late night reconnaissance inferred that he wanted to carefully inspect the poor condition of the city without the residents looking over his shoulder.

Some things are better done in private.

Maybe Nehemiah was an introvert and he preferred that time to himself. Whatever his reason, there were people in the city, lots of people, who wanted to know what was going to happen following his arrival with all his men.

Back to present day.

Back to you.

How do *your* followers feel when you are around? Does your proximity to them cause your employees or clients to be fearful, skeptical or curious?

When you are preparing for a big meeting or planning a course correction for your organization, do you hide in your office for days while you weigh options?

What are your people thinking and feeling when you are planning?

Or, how do they react when you are not sharing information?

If you don't know answers to these questions, I urge you to discover them. They are valuable insights for any leader when it comes to motivation, inspiration and collaboration in the workplace.

Introducing new ideas and plans is hard work. And risky.

Remember the last time you had a new idea? It may have involved a new solution to one of your organization's biggest problems or a new way to work with clients.

Question: What happened when you shared it with your staff for the first time?

List their various reactions. It will reveal a lot to you for future announcements, especially if you were inundated with the, *yeah, buts...*

Yeah, but we've never done it that way before. (curiosity)

Yeah, but we tried that before and it didn't work. (skepticism)

Yeah, but what if it has negative consequences for our company? (fear)

Then, there's the *timing* of your idea.

Share it too soon, and everyone with an objection jumps out of the woodwork to criticize and condemn it, listing all the reasons your new idea will not work.

On the other hand, if you hang on to an idea too long and *don't* share it, you run the risk of the idea being outdated or irrelevant before it even gets launched.

No matter when or how you share your Big Idea, some of your team members' emotions will be tempered by anxiety. Some will be curious and need more information. Some will be enthusiastic, eager and expectant. They sense something great will come of your plan.

Dealing with Curiosity

Fortunately, if your board, staff, and stakeholders are merely curious, getting them to buy into the Big Idea percolating in your head will probably be smoother than people who are skeptical or fearful.

A typical response might be voiced by one of your staff who is simply curious and wants to hear more about your Big Idea. Let's call her Curious Candace.

Curious Candace needs lots of <u>information</u>. She needs to be guided step-by-step through the journey you are about to launch.

At times, as a leader, you will need to be both cheerleader and father-figure. Curious Candace needs nurturing, coaching and a clear view of where you are going.

People like Curious Candace will ask questions. They will want assurance and even a practical set of steps to make your Big Idea a success.

As the leader, you need to be prepared to provide all or any answers they are seeking. Depending on your passionate proposal, you may not have all the answers yet.

So, be prepared to give as many answers as you can.

The nice thing about people like Curious Candace is that they usually remain curious even *after* you have explained most of the proposal.

Be patient.

By having to go back through all your explanations you may discover better answers and a more excellent set of plans because all that curiosity caused you to work harder in explaining and selling it.

This deepening process will add more credibility and validation to your Big Idea with all kinds of groups, including board members, staff, volunteers, clients and stakeholders.

Dealing with Skepticism

A little while ago, when I mentioned the, *yeah-but's*, did someone's face came to your mind? Did you immediately think of them as soon as you read the word, *skeptical*?

When I consult with executive directors or pastors about the skeptical individuals in the organization, each and every one of these leaders has a name or face that surfaces immediately in their consciousness.

The good news is you probably know the skeptical individuals in your company, church or organization.

We'll call one of these people, Skeptical Sam. We all know him.

When you share a new idea, Skeptical Sam crosses his arms, leans back in his chair and projects the attitude, *Prove it!*

I sometimes feel there are a handful of people in every organization who grew up in Missouri, the Show-Me-State.

Skeptical Sam's family goes back generations. He was born, raised and continues to live in the proverbial, Show-Me-State of his mind.

Sometimes, Sam's body language is hugely overt and blatant; crossing his arms or rolling his eyes. Or, he tosses you a suspicious frown. Or, he may make eye contact between other skeptics in the room who are already conjuring up all the reasons this new idea will not work. Other times, he's more subtle and you don't see his skepticism, but you *feel* it. It fills the room.

There's never just one reason your Big Idea will not work. Skeptical Sam and his buddies will have several concerns, each one more discouraging than the next.

Your dilemma will be how to minimize their skeptical mindset so they can feel engaged, and become excited about your Big Idea.

Think about how you approached Skeptical Sam in the past. In my leadership style, I prefer to work with these types of individuals behind closed doors, not in a larger meeting environment.

I highly recommend that approach.

If this skeptic has been in your organization for any length of time, you can already anticipate many of the reasons and excuses that will surface about the idea.

By dealing with Skeptical Sam *privately* in a one-on-one situation, you'll be able to listen to him carefully without being distracted by how their attitude is impacting the rest of a larger meeting.

You will also be able to determine how your anticipated response to his skeptical mindset is being received.

Is Skeptical Sam buying in to your new idea as your conversation progresses?

In my experience, most skeptics are deeply logical and rational. The curiosity we previously talked about is filtered with the proverbial, glass-half-empty attitude.

However in most situations, as he is given <u>logical and rational facts and practical steps</u>, Skeptical Sam will ultimately lean toward the Big Idea as a new way of thinking he can endorse.

Once Skeptical Sam becomes a believer in your Big Idea? Hang on, because many times these individuals become your *strongest* advocate for you.

Dealing with Fear

Unlike Curious Candace and Skeptical Sam, Fearful Felipe is usually neither logical *nor* rational. You've probably seen this meme on social media:

FEAR:
F – Failure
E – Embarrassment
A – Anxiety
R – Rejection

Obviously, as a leader, you need to tread carefully when dealing with the Fearful Felipes of your organization.

Anyone who leans toward fearful behavior leans that direction in a variety of ways. Therefore, you as the leader need to be <u>flexible</u> and <u>prepared</u> as you respond to each of the four emotions listed above in the meme.

Remember, Fearful Felipe and his counterparts typically do not respond well to a rational and logical explanation. They are emotional people, not intellectual analysts.

You will need to discern which of the areas your Fearful Felipes are struggling with and deal with each person *individually*. If you try to address them as a group, they will feed on each other's paranoia.

You will need to help them work through their feelings of potential failure, embarrassment, anxiety or rejection. Your professional, eloquent presentation, talking points and PowerPoint slides will not communicate well with Fearful Felipe.

<u>Recognize and respect his personal feelings</u>.

Again, a one-on-one situation is usually much more effective in dealing with emotion driven individuals. By dealing with Fearful Felipe behind closed doors, or over lunch, you can help minimize his emotional response which sets him apart from his logical and rationally-driven co-workers.

This will minimize Fearful Felipe's anxiety of how he (or she) is being perceived by others in the organization. These people live for the approval of others.

You will also be demonstrating your *sincere* concern for how they personally perceive your new idea. It may cause them to feel like a failure, feel embarrassment, anxiety or rejection. Once you have assured them of their value and validated them as a professional, the two of you can construct a series of action steps that will encourage buy-in and ownership.

You have won them over.

Leading the Charge

In verses 17 and 18, Nehemiah finally holds his press conference. He tells everyone why he came to the Jerusalem. He shares that the King of Persia is the one who allowed him to visit with the sole purpose of rebuilding the city.

This intrigues me.

Given how God moved to get Nehemiah permission to journey to Jerusalem, including a leave of absence granted by the king, I assume that Nehemiah also publicly shared God's hand in his arrival to the city.

However, Nehemiah is speaking to a group of disenfranchised Jews who have not had a formal corporate worship process for 3-4 generations. I suspect many of them did not even know the laws and commands God set forth with Moses, nor did they care.

Ezra had tried to reinvigorate the people of Israel to rebuild the wall a few years previously and had miserably failed.

For whatever reason, Ezra had gained little traction in his efforts to succeed.

Now, a stranger arrives in the city, claiming God's favor and a plan to rebuild a wall that has been in ruins for 160 years. This period is a long, long time which meant that God's promises and His protection could only be shared through the verbal retelling of history by priests and prophets.

After so many years and no consistent, formal way of passing on God's word, only a handful of Israelites would have any knowledge of God's promises.

With no live witnesses or in-person motivation, it is more than a little remarkable that the recounting of lore and tradition would be such an influential motivation here.

Nehemiah captivated the residents of Jerusalem by recounting all the ways God had intervened and orchestrated his arrival in the city.

The press conference turned into a pep rally, with the crowd zealously supporting Nehemiah in his goal to make the new wall a reality.

Everyone seemed eager, pumped up and ready to help him...

Well, almost everyone.

Nehemiah 2:19

> But when Sanballat the Horonite, Tobiah the Ammonite official and Geshem the Arab heard about it, they mocked and ridiculed us. "What is this you are doing?" They asked. "Are you rebelling against the king?"

> I answered them by saying, "The God of heaven will give us success. We His servants will start rebuilding, but as for you, you have no share in Jerusalem or any claim or historic right to it."

Stay tuned; we'll discuss these three *yeah-buts* later.

But for now, the first, and perhaps biggest, Habitat for Humanity rebuild was just beginning.

It would take a miracle of God to make it work.

CHAPTER 4
WHO'S YOUR NEIGHBOR?
Nehemiah 3

I don't know about you, but sometimes chapters in the Bible confuse me. Lists of names, genealogies, families and their home towns are boring to read.

However, I firmly believe that even these lackluster sounding verses are meant to be read and considered. God has a purpose for every one of them.

> **All Scripture is inspired by God and is useful to teach us what is true and to make us realize what is wrong in our lives. It corrects us when we are wrong and teaches us to do what is right. (2 Timothy 3:16, NLT)**

Let's look at Nehemiah 3 in light of this powerful endorsement. We get a sense of the men and women who worked on the wall and the sections they were responsible for.

Nehemiah 3:1-5

> **Eliashib the high priest and his fellow priests went to work and rebuilt the Sheep Gate. They dedicated it and set its doors in place, building as far as the Tower of the Hundred, which they dedicated, and as far as the Tower of Hananel. The men of Jericho built the adjoining section, and Zakkur son of Imri built next to them.**
>
> **The Fish Gate was rebuilt by the sons of Hassenaah. They laid its beams and put its doors and bolts and bars in place. Meremoth son of Uriah, the son of Hakkoz, repaired the next section. Next to him Meshullam son of Berekiah, the son of Meshezabel, made repairs, and next to him Zadok son of Baana also made repairs. The next section was repaired by the men of Tekoa, but their nobles would not put their shoulders to the work under their supervisors.**

Was the purpose of these passages simply telling us who was involved in the rebuilding of the wall of Jerusalem or was there more of a motive? What does a list of volunteer construction workers tell us about how to live out our faith or about how to lead a church or ministry?

God led Nehemiah to record this very special part of rebuilding the wall around Jerusalem to reveal something to us.

What was it?

I believe there are several practical examples and ideas here that we can use today as we pursue our own personal faith in leading our ministries and organizations.

God Loves and Inspires People (and You Need to, Too)

Often, I get locked into systems, problems and daily foul-ups that distract and discourage me from getting my work done.

Can you relate?

As I read Nehemiah 3, which simply lists the names, places and families that prepared to rebuild the wall, I am encouraged that God wants us to know about these people. He wants us to remember that, rich or poor, big or small, influential or unnoticed, we are *all* part of His Plan for people coming to know Him as Savior and Lord.

This chapter was not just about building something; it was about renewing and building lives.

Our love for each other and the world should be our highest goal with the life God has graciously given us.

I get stuck in the daily work of an organization, sometimes forgetting that there is a loftier reason for what I'm doing.

I get bogged down in balance sheets, cash flow and computer upgrades. As a result, I lose sight of the hurting people around me. I find myself growing callous to the stories of pain and suffering of those we see daily on my television screen.

I become numb to the very emotion that drove me to work with non-profit organizations and ministries.

What if our hero, Nehemiah, lost his angst and fervor before even *reaching* Jerusalem? What if somewhere along the dessert trek from Susa, he bailed out and retreated to the comfort and prestige of his position at the palace?

I know as a leader, you get distracted and discouraged at times, too. Hopefully, you have several close confidants and friends to turn to during these moments.

Sometimes, I simply turn to what many would consider an obscure list of names, reminding me that God loves me, and that I am in Nehemiah 3, along with the builders of the wall.

Here are five practical ideas we can glean from this passage of names.

#1 - Everyone can pitch in and help (and needs to!)

Take a few minutes and read Nehemiah 3.

At a quick glance, you will see people of all walks of life grabbing tools and rocks from the rubble and joining in the work.

Priests, sons, families, goldsmiths, perfume makers, political officials, daughters, people from other towns (Zanoah, for instance), Levites and servants.

Quite a collection of everyday people, making a great city safe from attack. Heroes really.

I suspect your organization is made up of, and supported by, a group of dedicated volunteers from many neighborhoods and towns, professions and skill sets, temperaments and personalities.

How cool is it that all these people wanted to help build a broken down wall? As cool as it would be that so many people would want to help *you* in your efforts to solve a problem or meet needs in your community!

Be sure to be *grateful* for all your followers, helpers and volunteers.

On a practical level, think of Nehemiah 3 as your volunteer roll call.

Be creative and discover ways to find lists of people to further your passion in building something. Perhaps your organization has available church lists, naming volunteers in an annual report. Maybe you publicly recognize volunteers at a major banquet or other event during the year, another set of workers.

#2 - Leaders need to set an example!

> **Eliashib the high priest and his fellow priests went to work and rebuilt the Sheep Gate. They dedicated it and set its doors in place, building as far as the Tower of the Hundred, which they dedicated, and as far as the Tower of Hananel. (v. 3)**

The priests, devout holy men charged with the spiritual health and vitality of God's people, rolled up the sleeves of their robes and helped build part of the wall. That's leadership, folks!

Have you ever been in a group or organization where the *leader* was disengaged from the work that needed to get done?

If so, they were not leaders.

Have YOU ever been that kind of leader?

I do wonder, what were the priests up to prior to Nehemiah's arrival? Clearly, the spiritual life of the people living in and near Jerusalem was not in great shape. It seems apparent that many of the laws, traditions and observances that God had outlined were not being kept.

Why hadn't the priests launched this building campaign?

They were the spiritual leaders of their beloved city.

And, if they hadn't been leading the people the way they should have in the beginning, what was *now* motivating them to build?

Were they embarrassed that someone else had come from 800 miles away to launch a project that the priests should have initiated?

Don't let my personal cynicism cause you to lose focus on the fact that the priests *did* help build. Perhaps the priests were just as motivated and encouraged as the other residents in Jerusalem because they were stirred by Nehemiah's passion.

And, don't forget, the king of Persia approved Nehemiah's trip and building project. Any attempt by the priests, or anyone else for that matter, to rebuild Jerusalem prior to this moment in time would probably have been met with governmental interference and punitive actions against the priests and citizens of Jerusalem.

Remember, Ezra had earlier failed because of some of those issues.

As this scenario clearly points out, the leader needs to set the example. If you are a church pastor, do you spend so much time preparing your sermon that people only see you on Sunday mornings?

Sermon prep is not as important as people prep.

Do you make time to visit the nursery before the service to greet and thank your volunteers for their time, energy and influence in the precious lives of young children?

Did you step out of your office during the spring work day, to help paint, spread mulch, and pull weeds?

Get out there and work among your people. Your sermon is not going to be powerful because of syntax, alliteration and metaphors. Touching the hearts and souls of your people is the power that gives your words resonance and relevance. It is vital for your followers to see you active and involved in even mundane tasks.

That is your most powerful pulpit.

If you are a leader in a non-profit organization or ministry, how do your volunteers and staff see you?

Are you out of the office courting that next big donor?

Are you meeting board members for lunch, testing their response to a new event or software upgrade?

When was the last time you helped volunteers stuff envelopes for a big mailing or newsletter? How long has it been since you spoke with a client of your ministry?

When did you last visit a run-down neighborhood where many of your clients live?

Powerful and revealing questions.

I am writing and asking myself these questions as well!

Don't get me wrong, sermons are important. Meeting with current and potential donors is vital. Setting up a plan, mirroring Nehemiah's to build your ministry *wall* is time well spent.

People will hear our action *sermons* much more than our spoken ones. Followers will only respond to leaders who are willing to jump in, get dirty, and lay a few bricks.

#3 – People help closest to home, <u>physically</u> and <u>emotionally</u>.

This was the genius of Nehemiah's strategy; self-preservation. People were not rebuilding the wall primarily for the city of Jerusalem, but for themselves!

In verses 23 and 29, we read of Benjamin and Hasshub, Azariah and Meshullam. All these builders were working on sections of the wall in close proximity to their own homes.

In today's thinking, they were volunteering in their neighborhoods, a simple concept, yet not one that leaders always think about, strategy-wise.

We bring volunteers to our offices or church to help out. But, how often do we deliberately think how we might be able to engage our volunteers in *their* community?

Political campaigns from the local level all the way to presidential elections use people in their communities and neighborhoods to distribute fliers on candidates and voting issues.

Local neighborhood volunteers are vital for these efforts. How are you as a leader equipping your volunteers to engage in *their* neighborhoods?

That's OTHER-centered leadership at its finest.

The other part of this takeaway is linked to the emotions of your followers.

Clearly, everyone who volunteered to work on the wall had a passionate investment toward the work of rebuilding. I imagine a combination of God's Spirit, Nehemiah's rallying speech and years of discouragement all came together to spark a deep sense of optimism, hope, and determination.

Your volunteers are only as engaged as their heart and emotions. A leader needs to find ways to keep volunteers emotionally connected to your work. Not in a fake, insincere way, there is no honor in manipulating people.

But, finding ethical ways to remind your volunteers how they are vitally contributing to the Big Idea is noble and a tribute to your leadership.

#4 – No one was a pro.

Look at the list of people and professions of the builders in Nehemiah 3.

Priests, craftspeople and just plain folks. There was not a carpenter, mason or architect among them. As far as we know, there was not a single professional construction worker in the entire group.

Your volunteers and stakeholders do not need to be a professional to help. There may be tasks that need professional expertise; you can outsource them. In my experience, the vast majority of the daily work that needs done in many non-profit organizations and churches can be delegated to eager, willing, enthusiastic *volunteers.*

Takeaway #5 – People want to go above and beyond your expectations.

> **Next to them, the men of Tekoa repaired another section, from the great projecting tower to the wall of Ophel. Above the Horse Gate, the priests made repairs, each in front of his own house. (v. 27-28)**

Here are two groups that are so invested into the rebuilding project, they are helping out in a *second* gap in the wall!

The men of Tekoa had a rich history with Jerusalem.

Tekoa was a military outpost located about 12 miles south and east of Jerusalem. Many believe it was fortified by King Rehoboam as a first defender against armies trying to invade from the south.

Tekoa was a strategic city and undoubtedly helped to protect and support Jerusalem. And now, decades later, the men and women of Tekoa still felt an emotional attachment to Jerusalem and its welfare.

In fact, they were so committed to Jerusalem they helped rebuild at least two portions of the broken down wall.

Many of them undoubtedly even commuted to take part in the construction. There's no clear indication that they lived in Jerusalem at the time. They probably came from Tekoa after hearing of the good work Nehemiah had sparked there.

And, don't forget the priests…

In Nehemiah 3:1, we saw that the priests were active and engaged in helping rebuild the city. And now, they double-downed on their efforts and put their hands, hearts and energy to working on another section of the wall.

No matter what they were doing before Nehemiah arrived, these religious leaders were now clearly serving as powerful instigators and role models by going above and beyond their responsibility.

If you ever had any doubts about Nehemiah's ability to motivate others those thoughts should be dispelled here and now.

His contagious confidence was a tribute to the concept of infectious passion.

The wall was being repaired and rebuilt with each passing moment.

These were inspirational and exciting times!

CHAPTER 5
ENEMIES FOREIGN
Nehemiah Chapter 4

The other shoe drops…

Long ago, I came to an important realization. I am **not** the smartest person in the room. Even if I am leading the meeting, even if am *in charge*, I cannot assume I know everything about everything that we are discussing.

Let's take a look at a real smart guy…Isaac Newton.

He is going to set the stage for our next glimpse into Nehemiah's journey and adventure in Jerusalem.

You may remember Newton from high school physics. He's the 17th-century scientist who showed a lot of smart people they weren't the smartest people in the room, either. He developed several principles that have guided our thinking for nearly 300 years.

For example, take his third law: *For every action, there is an equal and opposite reaction.*

If a bug hits your windshield, the bug loses. This is a crude example of that particular law.

SPLAT!

Here's my interpretation for leaders:

For every good and worthwhile Big Idea, there is a negative reaction.

You've seen and experienced this before, right? In a nutshell, they are known as the **distractors**, the **disruptors** and the **detractors**.

There's always a reason why your idea, plan, strategy or event will not happen successfully. Usually, these people can give you many reasons, *it* cannot work. The details of what *it* is, doesn't really matter.

From their perch, it cannot and will not work, so don't bother trying.

So many critics out there.

Guess what?

Nehemiah had the same problem. He had a Big Idea from God, and people had rallied alongside him to begin rebuilding a burned-out, broken down city. And the critics came swarming in along with them.

Check out **Nehemiah, Chapter 4:1-3**

> **When Sanballat heard that we were rebuilding the wall, he became angry and was greatly incensed. He ridiculed the Jews, and in the presence of his associates and the army of Samaria, he said, "What are those feeble Jews doing? Will they restore their wall? Will they offer sacrifices? Will they finish in a day? Can they bring the stones back to life from those heaps of rubble—burned as they are?" Tobiah the Ammonite, who was at his side, said, "What they are building—even a fox climbing up on it would break down their wall of stones!"**

Sanballat had become Nehemiah's chief antagonist and critic, joined by his snide partner, Tobiah. We'll see them launch several different attacks against Nehemiah and the builders throughout the entire story.

Critics never build up, they only tear down. Perhaps Nehemiah's story is where the adage came from here.

I suspect you have an individual in your life that always seems to be disrupting the work you are trying to accomplish. If you are a leader with a Big Idea you can bet your bottom dollar that someone will always be trying to cut you down and slow your progress.

Unfortunately, it is a fact of life for a leader. Get out in front and organize a group for more than a few weeks and you'll identify your own **distractors, disruptors,** and **detractors.**

They are surely out there lurking in the brush.

In fact, Sanballat was livid about Nehemiah's mission. Rather than a throwaway comment, this was an emotional, all-out, bona fide RANT!

Various Bible translations use different words to characterize Sanballat's tone, attitude and defiance:

Very angry - New Living Translation
Furious, completely enraged - Amplified Bible
Angry, greatly enraged - English Standard Version
Furious, very angry - New American Standard Bible
Exploded in anger, vilifying the Jews - The Message

Uh, did I mention he was…ANGRY?

His reaction was over-the-top. Can't you just see that vein in Sanballat's forehead about to burst?!

Sanballat and Tobiah were high ranking governors who supervised the provinces surrounding Jerusalem. They had the authority of the king of Persia, the very same king that had authorized Nehemiah to go rebuild Jerusalem.

Nehemiah's convoy and entourage probably passed through the territories these men governed. Now, Nehemiah's Big Idea was *interfering* with their lives.

Governors had positions of power and influence. They set rates and collected taxes on behalf of King Artaxerxes. They also were permitted to keep a portion of the taxes for their own living and governing expenses.

Whether they were kind, benevolent governors, or evil, underhanded leaders (there were many in those days), they still held tremendous influence and power over the people living near Jerusalem.

Nehemiah, with his grandiose mission, was getting in the way.

The Bible talks about the Jews of this time period as a *remnant*. Other modern words for remnant include *leftover, remainder, residue, or scrap*. There had been a good reason for this definition, too.

The Jews had been conquered, defeated and taken away from their homes. Many were now slaves and servants of the ruling party. In the region around Jerusalem, Sanballat and Tobiah were the ruling party.

So, these officials, these servants of the king, were treating God's anointed as lower class, non-people.

However, Sanballat and his minions also knew the consequences to them if the Jews rallied behind Nehemiah and rebuilt the wall of the city. They knew the history of the people of Israel and their powerful armies.

Sanballat and Tobiah were threatened by the mere possibility of the wall being completed.

They also realized that if God's people united, confessed their sin, and found God's favor again, they, and the rest of the **distractors, disruptors, and detractors** would be out of a job.

A strong, unified Jewish army and economy would certainly mean the end of Sanballat's position, influence, leverage and power.

So, they did what most people do when they feel threatened…

They attacked.

They launched an opening tirade and a powerful salvo to get the upper hand. In this case, they used ridicule and criticism to distract and discourage the builders.

What are those feeble Jews doing? (v.2)

Right from the start, Sanballat questioned the very work the Jewish laborers were doing. And, he got in a jab by calling them feeble. He blatantly challenged their authority to be working on this project. Never mind that his boss, the king of Persia, had authorized the construction.

Sanballat was publicly calling them out on their motives and reasons for beginning their work.

Sanballat was using the social media of the day, face-to-face communication, to blast Nehemiah, the workers and the work.

Nehemiah's reaction?

Was he surprised that these governors were opposed to the rebuilding of the walls? After all, he had permission from the king, right?

What about his builders?

Didn't Nehemiah just tell them all about the king's favor for this project?

He had letters, an entourage, and timber from the king's forest. He had even held a press conference announcing his credentials.

Didn't that mean anything?!

Why is this guy Sanballat on our case?

Put yourself in Nehemiah's sandals. You've just launched your Big Idea. The Big Idea that God gave you. You've just started an incredibly exciting and meaningful project, only to have some joker criticize, challenge and condemn you.

And, it got worse.

Sanballat turned up the pressure.

> **Will they restore their wall? Will they offer sacrifices? Will they finish in a day? Can they bring the stones back to life from those heaps of rubble—burned as they are? (v.2)**

And like any gang of bullies, one person calling names just eggs on the others. Tobiah joins in with the verbal ridicule.

> **What they are building—even a fox climbing up on it would break down their wall of stones! (v.3)**

Sanballat, and his cronies, attacked the personal abilities of the builders. He mocked them as feeble, weak, frail, spineless and powerless, with no talent, expertise, ability or motivation to change their situation or lives.

How do you feel when someone criticizes you--especially when they are unjust and ignorant in their analysis of you and your work?

When they challenge your abilities, your motives are suspected, and your character questioned - how does that *feel?*

For me, nothing hurts more than when I get criticized unfairly, especially by people who know nothing of me and my assignment.

I imagine you feel the same way.

When I worked with a large, nonprofit educational group, we came under attack. It was ugly.

Conservatives who were essentially anti-public school began to criticize us and our programs in several states. They were claiming all sorts of false and untrue things about our leader, organizations and programs.

Schools using our teacher tools, and their leaders, were confronted and criticized. In a few small towns, there were public forums and heated debates, causing deep divisions among friends.

Many of these conservatives sat in the same row in church with me. I was personally appalled that, people who thought a lot like me were attacking a hard-working, ethical organization, and the important work we were doing.

These **distractors**, **disruptors**, and **detractors** made our lives difficult for months. We spent thousands of dollars and hundreds of staff hours just dealing with the criticism and backlash.

Time and energy that should have been spent on our organization's collective Big Idea – helping educators and parents work together on behalf of students – was spent fighting these accusations instead.

The end of the story is – we finally got our message out to a broad enough audience that the false accusations were seen as just that – false and untrue.

The small group that had been spearheading this effort against us lost their steam. But, in the middle of the criticism, it was discouraging and extremely difficult to keep focused on our mission, purpose and Big Idea.

We felt just like Nehemiah's men and women who were working hard to help rebuild a wall that belonged to them, built by their ancestors. Many were sacrificing their livelihood to rebuild the wall near their home.

At the very time they were giving so much, they are criticized and demeaned by very powerful and influential people.

Not just their abilities are ridiculed, but the very core of their identity--their faith, their families, and their heritage.

From my personal experience, I imagine many workers just wanted to quit. They felt punched in the gut. Who would blame them for laying down their tools and walking away?

But, a leader cannot just walk away when criticized. No matter when you were given the mantle of leadership you *stay* with it.

Remember, the God of the Universe placed a Big Idea in your heart and life. You cannot ignore it or slip away into the night when someone doesn't like it.

As a new leader, you may understandably feel like walking.

Don't.

This is bigger than you; this is about Him.

> *What God initiates; He orchestrates.* – Pastor Andy Stanley

You will need to stand on God's promises and be fortified by close friends and co-workers. Your initial reaction of flight needs to be transformed into FIGHT.

God's way.

Think back to Nehemiah, Chapter 1 when Nehemiah prayed God's promises back to his Father? You will need to find a way to remind yourself that this is God's Idea, not yours.

I've kept a notebook to write down the events, situations and conversations that led me to my Big Idea. I regularly review this notebook to remind myself that this is not *my* idea.

It's God's Idea.

Let's take a closer look at how Nehemiah dealt with **distractors**, **disruptors**, and **detractors**. We see meaningful, practical steps for us as leaders today.

Poise

One of the remarkable assets of a leader is the poise they exhibit under pressure, the ability to stay calm and under control when a situation becomes desperate. Being prudent, staying calm, evaluating every aspect of the danger around him or her is a remarkable behavior and Nehemiah possessed it.

The Bible is filled with spiritual men and women of faith who exercised a coolness of faith under extreme pressure and threatening situations…

David standing calmly as he faced Goliath;

Shadrach, Meshach, and Abednego in the fiery furnace;

Daniel in the lion's den;

Esther exposing Haman's treachery;

Mary Magdalene quietly washing the feet of Jesus under intense scrutiny from the critical disciples;

Jesus as he was arrested in Gethsemane…On and on and on, we see leaders keeping their cool and obeying God in times of absolute pressure.

Nehemiah was no exception.

He had a calling to rebuild a wall and no governor, critic, **distractor, disruptor or detractor** was going to ruffle him. It was time for him to take his faith to a new level.

Upward.

Prayer

Nehemiah 4:4-5

> **Hear us, our God, for we are despised. Turn their insults back on their own heads. Give them over as plunder in a land of captivity. Do not cover up their guilt or blot out their sins from your sight, for they have thrown insults in the face of the builders.**

A great start for him and also for us.

You probably noticed that was a fairly short prayer.

Is that all?

Well, yes.

Let's look at Nehemiah's words as he prayed. Remember he was feeling sick and despondent back in the first chapter, when he fasted and prayed for four months. But, it was a deeply emotional prayer to an all-powerful God.

I think Nehemiah was as angry and frustrated here as he was sick in Chapter 1. The emotions and feelings expressed by Nehemiah were similar to some of King David's Psalms.

Heart-wrenching, passionate, desperate.

Powerful praying is not measured by quantity, but by quality, from-the-soul quality. How often do you pray this way?

Do you ever just let it all hang out to God? Do you let out every feeling, anxiety, frustration, and even an angry word once in a while! In our polite, politically-correct world, we struggle with praying honestly. We hold back on our prayers, because God may not like our tone.

Or, the people we are praying with might think less of us. David's Psalms were honest, transparent, and deeply emotional. He wasn't praying for *show*. He was sending his heartfelt pleas to a Sovereign God.

I also find it interesting that this time Nehemiah didn't pray and fast for four months like he did back in the capital city of Susa. The situation was different, and the timing had to be different, too.

He had to pray and get on with the work – the Big Idea. Kind of a, *Let's get this wall built*, prayer!

It's okay to be emotional with God.

We were created as emotional beings. Tell God how you're feeling, especially in the middle of someone criticizing the Big Idea He gave you.

It's not like God was surprised by the attack, even if you were.

He knew there would be opposition. Now that you are in the middle of it, you do, too.

So, let's do something about it, sooner than later. Nehemiah did.

Preparation

At that point, the walls had been rebuilt to about half of their total height
(v. 6). Just long enough for the builders to get tired and fatigued with the
work. They still had the second half to go.

The newness of the project was long gone and this now felt like actual
work. Because, it was…actual…work. It was just the right time for
distractors, **disruptors**, and **detractors** to swoop in with their naysaying
attacks and criticisms.

But, those would only work on a human level.

It appeared that the fact the builders kept working just infuriated Sanballat
and his comrades even more. So, Sanballat re-doubled his onslaught and
cranked up the threats and pressure.

Check out this ramped-up onslaught in **Nehemiah 4:11-12**

> **Also our enemies said, "Before they know it or see us,**
> **we will be right there among them and will kill them**
> **and put an end to the work." Then the Jews who**
> **lived near them came and told us ten times over,**
> **"Wherever you turn, they will attack us."**

Now, the region Sanballat governed was mostly to the north of Jerusalem.

Tobiah the Ammonite was the governor of the region just east of
Jerusalem. It is now the site of the city of Amman, Jordan.

The third group mentioned, the people of Ashdod, live in the area just west
of Jerusalem.

Surrounded.

The workers in Jerusalem, all volunteers and many unskilled in
construction, were surrounded by **distractors**, **disruptors**, and **detractors.**

Their work and their lives were being threatened.

The rumor mill predicted an attack at night. If you were working on the
wall, it didn't matter where in the city you worked, you were going to be
attacked by the biggest, meanest armies in the region.

The verbal threats were now physically real.

How would *your* volunteers fare in a time of great fear, threat and intimidation?

How would you handle this imminent crisis?

In the middle of Sanballat's rants, threats and coercion, it was amazing that Nehemiah didn't strike back. I respected his self-control, which is a fruit of the Holy Spirit.

Isn't that what we want to do when someone criticizes us?

Our natural response is to defend ourselves and lash out. We feel the blood rush from our neck to our face. Our ears get hot and red. Our heart beats faster and harder. Our breath quickens and our fists clench tightly as our blood pressure rises.

When we are attacked and criticized, our *first* reaction is to hit back. Flame the person on social media. Call them names. Deflect the criticism and point the accusation at someone else. Blame someone or something else.

Not Nehemiah.

God's Big Idea for him is getting jammed. The threats are beginning to influence the workers. There's now the reality of a military attack to kill or capture the builders.

The very threat that dispersed the People of God in the first place, hundreds of years ago, is now about to repeat itself.

Talk about discouraging.

But, Nehemiah did not lash back at Sanballat and his goons. He quietly prayed and prepared.

Are you writing this down?

How did he prepare?

He set up a defensive position inside the city, using the workers as his militia. He mentally armed his people with a strategy to defend themselves if Sanballat pressed military action.

Nehemiah took his plan three necessary steps further...

Everyone was equipped with a weapon and kept it handy while they worked. An alarm system was set in place, to alert all the workers if an attack occurred. The system told them exactly where to go in the city in the event of an attack.

He was not only a smart leader, he was a realistic one.

Nehemiah stayed close to the early warning system, a worker with a trumpet, so Nehemiah, as the leader, could determine the seriousness of any threat or attack. Then, with all of the workers now armed, they could gather at the place in the wall.

Some historians speculated that Sanballat's threat was empty. After all, Sanballat was governor of his region because of King Artaxerxes and remember, Artaxerxes was the same king who commissioned Nehemiah to rebuild Jerusalem in the first place.

If Sanballat attacked Nehemiah and the workers, he would have to explain to his powerful boss *why* he attacked the king's emissary.

Apart from that, Sanballat's anger and rage at Nehemiah and the workers was very real. His power, influence and leverage was going to be destroyed if the wall was rebuilt and the Jewish nation was restored.

Sanballat perhaps finds himself torn between attacking the king's emissary, and yet not wanting to give up his power. So, he is not even close to giving up.

Maybe Nehemiah discerned this early on, and was reasonably confident that there was no real attack coming. The story just doesn't give us enough information to know for sure.

Whether Sanballat was bluffing or not, Nehemiah had to address the situation with his workers.

His show of leadership and action worked. Sanballat's threats were exposed as empty. Jerusalem was never attacked, and Nehemiah's Big Idea moved forward.

How do we, as leaders today, deal with **distractors, disruptors,** and **detractors?**

Poise...Prayer...Preparation

Are you listening, leaders?

Live and learn – and lead.

CHAPTER 6
ENEMIES DOMESTIC
Nehemiah 5

Famine in the land.

When I was in elementary school, I had two good friends whose families were Jewish. I spent a great deal of time in my childhood with Joe and Mike.

Joe's family lived in the housing addition next door to mine, across a ravine. Joey and I would ride bikes, play army down in the ravine and fish from the bank of a river that was a short walk away.

Mike and I listened to music, read books, and watched Saturday morning cartoons in his bedroom. At the time, Mike was the only person I knew my age who actually had a television in his bedroom.

Very cool.

We grew up in very different faith traditions, yet I got along great with Mike and Joe and their families. They gave me a glimpse into their Jewish heritage, customs and beliefs.

I would observe and participate as best I could during their evening prayers and, of course, their Hanukkah rituals during that time of year.

One thing I observed about Mike's and Joe's moms was the manner and demeanor of a Jewish mother. At the risk of offending someone for overgeneralizing, I got to experience a stereotypical Jewish mom lived out in both these wonderful ladies.

They were hospitable, polite, loyal and pleasant almost to a fault. I felt like one of their kids when I was in their home.

They treated me with great respect and love.

I also saw and experienced the protective side of a Jewish mother if anyone dare cross or mistreat her son. Loyal and loving. Polite and protective. Friendly and fierce.

Here are a couple of truisms you may have heard related to moms and family life.

If momma ain't happy, ain't nobody happy.

When the queen bee is mad, the whole kingdom is sad.

These are maxims that describe my boyhood Jewish friends and their families perfectly.

With that background from my childhood, let's look into Nehemiah, Chapter 5 and follow an interesting development in not only the rebuilding of the wall, but also the dynamics of the Jewish workers.

Nehemiah 5:1-5

> **Now there arose a great outcry of the people and of their wives against their Jewish brothers. For there were those who said, "With our sons and our daughters, we are many. So let us get grain, that we may eat and keep alive." There were also those who said, "We are mortgaging our fields, our vineyards, and our houses to get grain because of the famine."**
>
> **And there were those who said, "We have borrowed money for the king's tax on our fields and our vineyards. Now our flesh is as the flesh of our brothers, our children are as their children. Yet we are forcing our sons and our daughters to be slaves, and some of our daughters have already been enslaved, but it is not in our power to help it, for other men have our fields and our vineyards.**

The story shows there's been some sort of famine, perhaps weather related, at the same time that Nehemiah has arrived in Jerusalem with his Big Idea.

Nehemiah arrived on the scene in late spring. Many of the Jewish workers who had been tending to their crops and fields have all come to Jerusalem to help Nehemiah rebuild the wall.

Their farms have been left largely unattended. They missed a key planting time to get crops in the ground, because they are laboring to build the wall.

So, there's a double whammy here.

No crops in the ground and long-term dire weather conditions. No food is a major issue, right? The work on the wall is preventing normal, everyday life from continuing.

This crisis had resulted in many of the workers not having the money they needed to purchase food, or pay their taxes, or cover other living expenses.

The wall was going forward while the family finances were spiraling downward.

One step forward; two steps back. This was not the American dream; this was a Jewish nightmare.

An interesting cultural custom of the day permitted, and even encouraged, the common practice of offering *family members* as payment for crops.

There wasn't really a monetary system in place. You couldn't just go to the bank or an online website and apply for a loan.

As a famer in the arid Middle East, you probably had a small plot of land, just enough for your family, a few neighbors, and maybe a little left over for trading.

You didn't have a huge bank account or a large stash of cash hidden under your bedroll. You traded your grain, livestock and other assets for what you needed to survive.

If you didn't have grain or livestock to trade with, you bartered your children. As strange as it seems to us, it was a normal custom of the day.

Many translations of the Bible use the word *sell* when referring to this sort of transaction.

However, it really was more of a loan arrangement. Think of one of the popular pawn shop shows on TV these days.

It's hard to think that with a straight face. But back in the day, it was a reality.

For instance, jump in your Bible to Genesis, Chapter 29. Check out the love story of Jacob and Rachel. Rachel's father, Laban, agreed to their marriage, as long as Jacob worked for Laban for seven years (giving a whole new definition to the term, "tough love").

Jacob fulfills his obligation and earns Rachel as a wife.

Jacob and Rachel's story demonstrates that the bartering of children was a common and well-used practice at the time. When your kids served their time or when you had enough grain or livestock to trade, your children were released from service and returned to their family.

Think about that for a moment.

How would you feel if it had been you, as a teenager helping your family with attending a few cattle and a few meager acres of land?

You probably knew the custom and tradition and the reason your father was asking you to work for someone else. He knew that eventually you would return to your family, and probably increase your family's reputation, assuming you did a good job.

But, Jewish parents having to farm out their kids while working on the wall, just exacerbated an already difficult situation.

The story also states there were some Jewish pawn brokers (landowners) charging interest, in addition to having other people's children work for them.

This was strictly against Jewish Law and custom, adding insult (and interest) on top of injury.

Sons were being loaned out. Daughters were being loaned out. Crops weren't in the ground. There would be no food for the winter, even if the walls were rebuilt in time.

There just wasn't enough to go around. All because of Nehemiah's wall.

The Jewish mothers and grandmothers explode.

In my childhood, I got a small glimpse of the defending passion of Jewish moms when I visited my friends, Joe and Mike.

I can only imagine hundreds of these mothers standing by the wall, glaring at Nehemiah and their husbands as they tried to carry out their mission of building.

Talk about a PR nightmare!

I know I would not have wanted to be in Nehemiah's sandals at this point.

In the previous chapter, we saw Nehemiah avert threats from Sanballat, Tobiah, and Geshem. Now, Nehemiah has a whole region of Jewish moms and grandmothers after him.

From the frying pan into the fire. Trouble on the home front was far scarier than anything from the foreign enemies.

Believe it.

The next section describes how Nehemiah began to handle the situation. He responded in the way he always responded.

He went off by himself to pray and commune with God.

This reflected a leadership principle for all of us to follow.

Sometimes, you need to get away from everyone and meditate on the Big Idea God has planted in you.

Think about the times Nehemiah went off by himself to think about, and then act on, the Big Idea God places in his heart

He demonstrated that in Chapter 1, when he fasted and prayed for four months.

He did it again in Chapter 2, when he went off to inspect and survey the crumbling walls of Jerusalem before announcing the Big Idea to the people.

And, here it is, *déjà vu* all over again.

Spiritual leadership, folks.

> **I was very angry when I heard their outcry and these words. I took counsel with myself…(Neh. 5:6-7)**

I tend to be fairly reflective in most areas of my life. I do plenty of navel-gazing before I share my thoughts and feelings with people.

Sometimes my family wishes I'd talk more, instead of think more.

I eventually get around to sharing what's in my head and heart, but it takes a while.

I relate to Nehemiah in so many ways as I see how he was thoughtful and contemplative in his approach to life's challenges.

I'm sure that's why this book of the Bible has meant so much to me over the years.

Nehemiah thinks to himself (again) to consider how God is going to work out and resolve this dilemma.

After all, if God puts a Big Idea in your heart, he's going to provide solutions and course-corrections to whatever is preventing the Big Idea from getting accomplished.

Go Private Before Going Public

Everyone loves the dramatic last minute touchdown to win a championship, but no one ever talks about the strategic and private *huddle* that set it up.

Nehemiah takes council with himself, thinking through how to address this volatile situation.

How do you calm anxious, angry mothers?

Even Nehemiah was angry, but rather than let his emotions overtake him, he got alone and took it up with the wise and self-controlled Holy Spirit.

I think he bluntly shared his own thoughts and feelings and let the Holy Spirit temper them and guide him.

Nehemiah submitted his frustration and anger to the soothing heart of God before launching into a public solution.

Nehemiah calls a family meeting. Well, more like a family trial as the verse states here.

> **I took counsel with myself, and I brought *charges against* the nobles and the officials. (v. 7,** italics mine)

Brought charges. Legal language. Public charges.

Most commentaries indicate the landowners and nobles were just engaging in a blatant shakedown of the families rebuilding the wall. I can, for the most part, go along with that reasoning.

Remember, it's been more than 150 years since God's people were worshiping together in the city of Jerusalem, resulting in several generations of not following God's Law.

They'd had many decades of assimilating into the culture and lifestyle of the nations that conquered them. Maybe the pawnshop behavior wasn't as blatant and notorious as some believe.

Still, Nehemiah knew that the motivation or mindset of the people wasn't the most important factor.

What was important is the fact the famine was causing hardships.

These hardships were pressured by the loaning and pawning of sons and daughters because families couldn't pay their taxes.

They could get food and seed from those that had it, but only by paying with their children.

Many times, as a leader, you will need to decipher peoples' motives.

You'll need to sort out whether a board member's overactive involvement is driven by honest concern for the organization, or purposeful meddling. Is a volunteer's negative comment genuine, or an attempt to undermine one of your staff members?

Unacceptable.

You must be discerning and then courageous in your confrontation towards that individual.

If behaviors and actions are distracting and contaminating the Big Idea, you will need to handle it.

Manage it.

Deal with it.

Nehemiah dealt with his situation very publicly because it was a very public issue. Not every issue needs a family meeting. Issues need to be addressed with an *appropriate* level of privacy or publicness.

Nehemiah knew this issue needed to be addressed publicly…and in person. A memo or post on social media would not suffice.

A big, public problem demands a big, public solution.

Make a note.

He essentially delivered a courtroom-style argument, outlining the problem and how it needed to be solved. Here's my paraphrase:

Hey, you guys. Isn't it bad enough we are already in slavery and captured by Babylonians, and now you are making it worse!

I know, because I work for the king. With this famine causing even more problems, you disgrace us, and our God, even more by overcharging Jews, people of your own bloodline, for their taxes, land, food and seed.

Worse, you are making your own people pay interest, a practice forbidden by God's law.

Humble yourselves and stop now or Almighty God will turn His back on you. Give back everyone's land and children – now! You need to fall to your knees in obedience to Him and make amends or the priests in God's holy Temple will make sure you are held accountable and not do this ever again.

Nehemiah's large and very public family meeting worked and the people got back to work on God's Big Idea.

Amen.

CHAPTER 7
DO THE RIGHT THING (ALL THE TIME)
Nehemiah 5:14-19

Always do right. This will gratify some people and astonish the rest.
– Mark Twain

Great quote by one of America's best-loved storytellers. Mr. Twain knew that people didn't always do the right thing, even in his day. We sometimes think that the current time we live in is the only one that's full of negativity, dishonesty, venom and lies.

Nope.

It's been that way since Adam and Eve lived. And it will continue this way until the world ends.

People cheat. Lie. Steal. Take advantage of others. Manipulate.

And, now, you get to be a leader in this mess. Let's try to bring some light out of all this darkness. I am with you here.

So was Nehemiah.

In his day, he had to deal with Sanballat and his cronies who abused their rank and position as governors.

In the previous chapter, we saw how even the Jews were manipulating their own family and heritage by bartering family members and charging interest.

More darkness. And, it continues today.

Just take a peek at any, and I mean *any*, newspaper headline or internet newsfeed. In *every* sector of society, we see moral failure and disgrace in politics, education, business, entertainment and sports.

We are an equal-immoral-opportunity society. Scandal. Embezzlement. Fake news. Smear campaigns.

All because we are, well, *human*.

Do not naively think the nonprofit and organized religious world are immune from this lack of character and bad behavior. As a leader, you will most likely find people in your organization and ministry who lie, cheat, manipulate and abuse with the best (or worst) of them.

Or, they may be people who are connected to your Big Idea: vendors, suppliers, printers, and other stakeholders. It will take many shapes and forms. It will show its ugly head at the worst possible moment.

But it WILL show up. Basic human nature. Looking out for #1.

Their mantra is scarily obvious, *I'm putting my needs, wishes, desires and demand above and ahead of others.*

Don't be *that* leader!

Let's dive back into Nehemiah's story and see how he handled human nature in his time.

> **Moreover, from the time that I was appointed to be their governor in the land of Judah, from the twentieth year to the thirty-second year of Artaxerxes the king, twelve years, neither I nor my brothers ate the food allowance of the governor. The former governors who were before me laid heavy burdens on the people and took from them for their daily ration forty shekels of silver. Even their servants lorded it over the people. But I did not do so, because of the fear of God. I also persevered in the work on this wall, and we acquired no land, and all my servants were gathered there for the work.**
>
> **Moreover, there were at my table 150 men, Jews and officials, besides those who came to us from the nations that were around us. Now what was prepared at my expense for each day was one ox and six choice sheep and birds, and every ten days all kinds of wine in abundance. Yet for all this I did not demand the food allowance of the governor, because the service was too heavy on this people. Remember for my good, O my God, all that I have done for this people. (Nehemiah 5:14-19)**

Nehemiah has been appointed governor of Judah, the region surrounding Jerusalem. Not only is he spearheading the Big Idea God gave him, he has now been selected by the king of Persia to serve in an official role.

His faithfulness and moral character was so undisputed, he was made the official leader for this city and immediate surroundings.

As governor, Nehemiah was entitled to certain perks and benefits of a political leader. Perks are important and necessary to leaders.

The U.S. President gets to fly on Air Force One. A state governor usually moves into a mansion in the capital city. A university president gets housing on campus.

The perks and benefits are not usually unreasonable. Given the 24/7/365 nature of those jobs, it makes sense to have housing which makes that job easier.

Can you imagine the US President flying a commercial airline?

Peanuts or pretzels, Mr. President?

Think of the havoc!

Or, what if state governors had to rent hotel meeting space for all their appointments? The energy and time to get work done this way would be debilitating.

I believe some perks are important for leaders. Let's face it, Nehemiah was the leader – the governor. He deserved some bennies.

He didn't take them. None. Nada. Zip. Zilch.

Call it moral authority. Call it strong character. Call it ethical courage. Call it crazy. Most of us would love a perk – any perk – in our jobs.

Whatever term you use, he worked doubly hard to set an example of integrity and honesty.

Nehemiah was going to make sure that his administration served the people well. He was going to do the right thing, no matter what.

After all the people of Jerusalem had been through, and were still going through, this was the only way Nehemiah knew how to behave.

As governor, he could use an allotment of taxes for his own food and provisions, and for his household and staff.

But he didn't do it.

He had every right to draw down on public funds to run his public office.

Nope. Not Nehemiah.

He used his own fund. His money. His resources.

He was going to make sure that no one could slander, accuse, or threaten his leadership. He was going to do the right thing.

This surely astonished many.

An honest question is how can Nehemiah afford to feed 150+ people – *every* day? A banquet feast for dozens each and every day. Great question.

In my background reading for this book, I came across a listing of salaries for Assyrian officials. Different kingdom, but in a same general time period as Nehemiah's time.

The cupbearer was listed as the fourth highest paid staffer in the kingdom, even more highly paid than the Supreme Court justices of the day.

So, a cupbearer in those days was highly trusted, greatly respected and handsomely rewarded. High risk – high reward.

My assumption is Nehemiah used his own money, saved from his cupbearer salary, to provide this daily feast for the masses. The people had been so abused and repressed over time, that Nehemiah knew the only right thing to do was to cover this out of his own pocket.

He did the right thing. Just like Mr. Twain advised several centuries later.

The right thing.

During my professional career, I've had several opportunities to do the right thing. Hopefully, I've done that more often than not. Let me share a couple of situations.

I'm changing names, to protect the innocent (and the guilty).

Amanda was the president of a large nonprofit organization I worked for, and Rita was the head of marketing. Rita came to us with a strong background in working with large, for-profit educational companies.

Nothing wrong with that, but she was not used to working in a collaborative culture.

Collaboration and cooperation tends to slow decisions. It takes more time for things to get done. More people are involved in meetings and conversations.

Amanda and Rita locked horns pretty much from day one, in my view. Amanda was working hard to steer our organization, and was wisely dealing with the culture of slower, more deliberate decisions.

Rita, I think, found this inefficient and cumbersome. She was used to fast-paced, high-energy, *get-it-done* atmosphere.

Can you see these two trains, the fast-paced express and the slow-moving freight, on a collision course here?

I worked in Rita's division, although I wasn't a direct report. One evening, Rita called me at home (not a customary practice). She told me she was going to confront Amanda in the morning at the weekly executive leadership team meeting.

She was going to challenge Amanda's competency and threaten to resign (if Amanda didn't let Rita do things her way).

Down the tracks they came. This was going to get ugly.

Why Rita bothered to call several of us involved in the situation the night before to broadcast her next move is still a mystery to me. I suppose an attempt to get us on her side and hope that we would be in her court.

And, why she would make this threat in *public*, in front of other executives also escapes me to this day.

One thing I learned early in my work-life with my supervisors is the mantra, *No surprises.*

Don't let your supervisor or manager get sideswiped by information, good or bad. They need to hear it from *you* first.

As a result, I believed I needed to do something. Publicly threatening the organization's top leader wasn't right. Amanda needed to be informed of the coup bearing down on her.

Amanda was a very private person, and I did not have her home phone number. (This was in the dark ages – before cell phones.) However, I did know Amanda's assistant.

I called her and raised the flag that Amanda was walking into a trap.

The next morning, Amanda, after having been alerted by her assistant, canceled the weekly meeting, in which Rita was going to confront her, and invited Rita to her office.

Amanda called her bluff and asked for her resignation letter.

Caught completely off guard, Rita had no choice but to resign and leave. Amanda had upstaged Rita's end-game. Amanda outplayed the player.

> **See that no one repays evil for evil, but always seek after that which is good for one another and for all people. (1 Thessalonians 5:15)**

My only perk in this potential debacle was a big hug from Amanda, thanking me for giving her a heads-up. Since Amanda wasn't a hugger and rarely showed personal appreciation, her hug was a big deal and very appreciated.

The footnote to this story is that Rita, after essentially stepping into her own trap and forcing her own resignation, had the audacity to complain (in private) to the people she called the night before, alerting us that she was going to threaten to resign.

She was *shocked* and *astonished* that someone did the right thing and gave the boss a warning.

I did the right thing, and a poisonous employee moved to another job. I did the right thing, and got a hug for it.

I'm ok with that.

Doing the right thing is hard. But, as a leader in Nehemiah's day or in our day, it is imperative.

Another story from my life is a tragic situation at a local church.

I was serving on the elder board at the time, and we learned, over time, that our senior pastor was behaving inappropriately. We could have ignored it, or played it down and resumed ministry as usual.

Or, we could do the right thing.

We confronted him about the issue, and he denied it, despite several confirmed facts verifying his guilt.

After much discussion and prayer, we asked for his resignation letter, which he gave to us.

As a board of elders, we firmly (and prayerfully) believed we needed to be open and transparent about the reason for his departure.

This resulted in a number of extremely tense, volatile meetings with the entire congregation, and individuals. The elders were accused of forcing him out and not being caring enough as Christians to give him another chance.

We were accused by some of tearing him down as man and pastor.

Did we do the right thing?

> **But you, take courage! Do not let your hands be weak, for your work shall be rewarded. (2 Chronicles 15:7)**

As a team of church leaders, we were unanimous in our decision and how it was carried out. But, the public meetings were painful for everyone in the entire church.

I was asked to serve as moderator and facilitator for many of the meetings. As the messenger, many people took out their feeling on me personally.

It took many weeks, even months, for emotions to cool and for some people to talk to me again.

That was several years ago. That particular church is growing steadily and making an impact for Jesus locally, and around the world.

I believe God honored the faithfulness, integrity and transparency of that elder board. I was fortunate to be with a team of men committed to God's Truth and His local fellowship.

Yes, we did the right thing. If you seek out the truth in God's wisdom and purity, you will bring honor to Him and respect to your own reputation. And, to your organization and Big Idea.

Therefore, to the one who knows the right thing to do and does not do it, to him it is sin. (James 4:17)

Always do the right thing. You might get a hug, or you might get verbally slapped.

Either way, as a leader, you always need to do the right thing, whether protecting your supervisor, spiritually confronting a pastor, or rebuilding a wall.

You may not need to feed 150 people every day out of your own pocket. But, use Nehemiah's example to remind yourself daily about doing the right thing.

Always. Without fail.

It will be gratifying – and astonishing.

CHAPTER 8
GOOD NEWS AND OTHER NEWS
Nehemiah 6:1-19

The Good News

This next set of verses may be some of the most encouraging lines for me in the entire Bible. If you aren't of the same faith or beliefs as me, that's ok.

I still think you'll find this part of the story encouraging and reassuring. I could write an entire book just based off this chapter.

Now for the *spoiler alert* ...the wall is almost done. There are a few odds and ends to finish up and the city will be completely protected.

In the world of home remodeling and construction, these last few odds and ends are called a *punch list*. It's a time for the builder and client to go through the home or office and detail the little things that need done before everyone agrees the project is finished.

There are just a few gates to still hang **(v.1)**. But, the Big Idea that God placed and nurtured in Nehemiah's heart is nearly done.

Jump ahead to **Nehemiah 6:15. The wall was built in just 52 days!**

Have you ever been part of a building program for your organization? Or, tackled a remodeling job at your own home? If so, you know the joys, pains, problems and challenges that you encountered on your way to finishing your dream.

We did a relatively small remodel in our basement a few years ago, finishing off one room and a bathroom. It took longer than 52 days.

Based on what my wife and I went through, I can't even begin to comprehend the monumental task completed by Nehemiah. He was an amazing man for a daunting challenge.

We improved a room. He changed an entire *city!*

And, as the completion of the wall is imminent, the attacks and assaults increase. His enemies were digging in for their final assault on his vision, his Big Idea.

The Other News

Sanballat and his crew launched a last-ditch attempt to derail, discredit and delay Nehemiah from getting the punch list done. They're version of punching entails increasing their power, control, influence and leverage to the point of destroying a man of God and his mission.

Nehemiah's antagonists knew that if the gates are hung, there is no way to attack and invade the city of Jerusalem.

In ancient days, when an enemy attacked a fortified city, it was called a *siege*. The strategy was to surround the city and choke off the inhabitants from food, water and supplies of any kind.

At that point, the citizens would be in no condition to fight back when the sieging army launched their attack and would have no alternative but to surrender.

Word of a long, protracted siege of Jerusalem would certainly get back to King Artaxerxes and he would question why his subjects were attacking other Persians. As a result, Sanballat needed to act and get Nehemiah out of the way before all the gates were hung and the city completely secured.

Like a desperate boxer punching above their weight, Sanballat and his allies still wanted Nehemiah and the entire region to know they were driven to defeat Nehemiah, and his wall. They were not going away.

They've been fighting Nehemiah since he arrived in Jerusalem. They had changed their attacks and threats to try and find a gap in Nehemiah's plan and the lives of the builders without any luck.

It was desperation time for them.

They made three more attempts to bring down Nehemiah. If they couldn't bring down the wall, they planned on bringing down the man who brought this dilemma to them.

They began by sending a letter to Nehemiah.

They wrote:

> **It is reported among the nations, and Geshem also says it, that you and the Jews intend to rebel; that is why you are building the wall. And according to these reports you wish to become their king. And you have also set up prophets to proclaim concerning you in Jerusalem, 'There is a king in Judah.' And now the king will hear of these reports. So now come and let us take counsel together.**

Nehemiah replied:

> **Then I sent to him, saying, "No such things as you say have been done, for you are inventing them out of your own mind." For they all wanted to frighten us, thinking, "Their hands will drop from the work, and it will not be done." But now, O God, strengthen my hands. (Nehemiah 6:6-9)**

The letter is frankly a series of false threats, intended to dissuade Nehemiah from his goal. In today's terms – fake news.

They claim Nehemiah clearly is going against the king. Nehemiah wants to be the ruler. Nehemiah is going to have people announce him as king.

Blah, blah, blah.

Sanballat is desperate.

This is the fifth letter like this that Sanballat and his cronies have sent. Five! They are not getting a rise out of Nehemiah, so they figure they'll just be louder. More is better. If one letter didn't work, then we'll send more.

Media bullying.

I love this Albert Einstein quote…

Insanity is doing the same thing over and over again and expecting different results.

Sanballat and his followers are insane. Their tactics match their madness.

If it's not working, do it some more, just louder, faster, and maybe something will stick. Please, please, do not be this leader.

Also, it's important to note that this fifth letter was an open letter. In the ancient world, important letters and communiques were sent rolled up or folded. It was customary for the sender to use a wax seal to secure the letter. The seal usually had their kingdom's crest or symbol on it, verifying the sender was legitimate.

Think secure, encrypted email.

Since Nehemiah never reacted to the first four letters, Sanballat decided to not seal his fifth note. You can assume that every courier and messenger along the way, just *happened* to open and read the letter.

That's just curious human nature.

It goes without saying that as soon as one person saw the note, a lot of others also saw it or learned of the letter's content.

Sanballat used the Twitter or Instagram feed of the day to make sure everyone – and I mean everyone, could see the content of his letter. It was no longer a personal note to Nehemiah; it was a media campaign to involve as many people as possible.

Sanballat was so desperate, he needed to get others on his side.

He needed to convince other people with his fake news. He needed to plant doubt in other people's minds about Nehemiah and his motives.

One cannot blame Sanballat for trying. He gets an *A* for effort and enticement. Face it, he also believes in his cause and has passion to follow through on it.

But, he is fighting against God. He has no chance to win this battle. God has His hand on Nehemiah, the good and faithful servant who has been trusting God with all things.

Nehemiah is laser-focused on the Big Idea God has given him. Sanballat, or any other opponent for that matter, has no power here. The wall is going to be rebuilt.

The five letters don't work. Nehemiah doesn't flinch. He doesn't blink. He continues to work through his punch list in order to complete the wall, making Jerusalem secure.

As a leader, have you ever felt like someone is using fake news, made-up stories and accusations against you?

Yeah, me too.

As long as you are in a leadership role (and making a positive impact) this is very likely to happen to you. It may not be as public and intense as the fake news and accusations Nehemiah faced, but don't be surprised if it happens to you and your Big Idea. Be prepared for it.

Sanballat decides (finally) that if open, public letters with fake news aren't going to shake Nehemiah, he'll try something more subtle.

Why not?

He's tried everything else, right? He's losing. So he turns to his companion in crime, Tobiah, to launch this next attack.

> **Now when I went into the house of Shemaiah the son of Delaiah, son of Mehetabel, who was confined to his home, he said, "Let us meet together in the house of God, within the temple. Let us close the doors of the temple, for they are coming to kill you. They are coming to kill you by night." But I said, "Should such a man as I run away? And what man such as I could go into the temple and live? I will not go in." And I understood and saw that God had not sent him, but he had pronounced the prophecy against me because Tobiah and Sanballat had hired him. For this purpose he was hired, that I should be afraid and act in this way and sin, and so they could give me a bad name in order to taunt me. Remember Tobiah and Sanballat, O my God, according to these things that they did, and also the prophetess Noadiah and the rest of the prophets who wanted to make me afraid. (Nehemiah 6:10-14)**

I love to read. One of my favorite topics to read is Cold War espionage and thriller novels. I enjoy non-fiction books from the US/Soviet Cold War time period. I'm not a fan of war and nuclear obliteration, but the time period, the cloak and dagger stories and historical figures have always fascinated me.

In spy jargon and folklore, a *mole* is an individual working inside your opponent's organization or company. I believe the inference here is that Sanballat has a mole inside the city of Jerusalem.

In fact, the mole is the son of a priest. Someone who is probably glad that Nehemiah came on the scene and is excited about the fact this Big Idea is making good progress. (Remember in Nehemiah, Chapter 3 when the high priest and priests all joined in and built a portion of the wall?)

Sanballat and Tobiah have a *mole* inside the city of Jerusalem and are going to try and cause Nehemiah to make a mistake and ruin his credibility, and undermine his leadership.

Good thing Nehemiah was steadfast in his judgement. He was not going to give in to another threat or temptation.

Nehemiah knew that if he entered the Temple, his entire reason for being in Jerusalem would be undermined. He would be safe in the Temple, while the workers were still out in the open, possibly under threat.

His leadership and authority would be irrevocably damaged.

Everything he had said and done up until this time would be questioned and scrutinized. The entire background and reason for building the wall would be suspect and under suspicion.

We'll see later in Nehemiah's story that Tobiah is connected to the Jewish high priest, probably through marriage. He uses this connection to forge contracts with other Jews and do business while still criticizing and attacking Nehemiah.

Tobiah uses his knowledge of Jewish law, and his contacts, to set a trap for Nehemiah.

Shemaiah, an apparent invalid, invites Nehemiah to come to his house. Shemaiah has some sort of prophetic gift and warns Nehemiah of a vision. He claims that people are coming to kill Nehemiah and the safest place to hide and be safe is the Temple.

There is an interesting piece of background to this quick set of verses.

Reread the phrasing:

> **Let us close the doors of the temple, for they are coming to kill you. They are coming to kill you by night. (v. 10)**

In the original language, this wording is close to a poem or song. It wasn't an offhand comment. It's scripted. Someone took time to compose a poem, almost a presentation, to try and convince Nehemiah that his life was in danger.

Think about it in today's terms. Someone wants to convince you of a threat or danger to you or your organization. They build a PowerPoint presentation and write a song to explain it to you. They are using the formality of song and verse to make their threat more important and convincing.

Would you bite? Would the packaging and presentation blur the facts of the message?

Or, in this case, the lack of *facts*.

Nehemiah doesn't bite; he doesn't even nibble. He sees through the glitz and recognizes that this is a set-up. Nehemiah doesn't follow their script.

Once again, Nehemiah sees the Big Idea, and stays focused on facts and truth. He is strong and direct (and speedy) in his response.

He confronts the issue directly, yet still humbly.

> **Should such a man as I run away? And what man such as I could go into the temple and live? I will not go in. (v. 11)**

Thankfully Nehemiah kept up his guard, the bell rings, and Nehemiah stays firmly positioned in the middle of the ring.

Sanballat stays on the ropes and is going down for the count.

But the fight isn't over quite yet.

As the final rounds unfold, we'll see how Nehemiah changes his leadership focus and embarks on Part 2 of the Big Idea.

Stay tuned.

CHAPTER 9
THE WORK HAS JUST BEGUN
Nehemiah 7:1-3

The wall is built! The City of Jerusalem is safe and secure!

Mission accomplished.

Now in most epic stories, our Hero, Nehemiah, would hop on a horse (or, in this case, a camel) and ride off into the sunset to a crescendo of dramatic music. Nehemiah can retire and live out his life in peace and quiet, proud and content in his once-in-a-lifetime achievement.

Uh, no.

He knows better. He's too smart for that.

Let's look back at Nehemiah, Chapter 1 for a hint of what Nehemiah is going to do next.

> **Remember the instruction you gave your servant Moses, saying, 'If you are unfaithful, I will scatter you among the nations, but if you return to me and obey my commands, then even if your exiled people are at the farthest horizon, I will gather them from there and bring them to the place I have chosen as a dwelling for my Name.' (Nehemiah 1:8, 9)**

Nehemiah's end game was never just the building of a wall. He knew the real security and prosperity for Jerusalem would only happen when the people of God began to again honor and be obedient to God Almighty.

Yes, the rebuilding of the wall was an event that excited and motivated people. It was a tangible, visible project that everyone felt through their smashed fingers, sore muscles and sweat.

This was never really about a building *project*; it was about building *people*. Nehemiah knew that God's promises were not attached to a *structure*. They were attached to *Scripture*.

God wasn't going to bless the People of Israel because they were good builders.

God would only bless them if they were faithful and obedient builders.

So, now that the city of God is secure, Nehemiah turns his energy and attention to rebuilding the *people* of God.

No easy task. The people of Jerusalem, and the Israelites in general, hadn't been a unified nation for more than 160 years. The numerous kingdoms that had conquered the Jewish people had scattered them across thousands of square miles.

Like Nehemiah, many had never even been to Jerusalem. How can people regroup after decades of living apart, spread over a vast territory?

Many historians believe that the first six chapters of Nehemiah are autobiographical. As we'll see in a minute, Nehemiah is getting ready to go back to Susa, and work for the king again.

He's stepping aside as the onsite, local leader, so we see a change in authorship and tone. It is not unexpected in this time period to have many authors documenting a story or series of events.

So while the writing is altered, the storyline and Big Idea do not change. Your people, projects and plans may change often.

Your Big Idea will not.

Nehemiah needed to make sure the plan and project continued moving forward. While the wall was built, the workers needed to be reminded that the work was not finished yet.

> **After the wall had been rebuilt and I had set the doors in place, the gatekeepers, the musicians and the Levites were appointed. I put in charge of Jerusalem my brother Hanani, along with Hananiah the commander of the citadel, because he was a man of integrity and feared God more than most people do. I said to them, "The gates of Jerusalem are not to be opened until the sun is hot. While the gatekeepers are still on duty, have them shut the doors and bar them. Also appoint residents of Jerusalem as guards, some at their posts and some near their own houses."**
> **(Nehemiah 7:1-3)**

Nehemiah has now stepped back and needed reliable, trustworthy leaders to take his place. He went to people he knew and respected. He called on his closest advisors to spearhead the next phase.

If you recall, Hanani was the person mentioned back in Nehemiah, Chapter 1, who came to Susa and gave Nehemiah a report on the status of Jerusalem. He's referred to as a brother.

Now, we do not know if he was a flesh-and-blood brother or simply a kindred-spirit, but obviously their relationship was sound and mutually respectful.

The kind of relationship *you* need to foster when you're the leader. It is absolutely critical that you identify who's going to be on your side when your Sanballat threatens and attacks you and your Big Idea.

In current-day terms, **Who's got your back?**

So, who's this Hananiah guy? How did the king's commander get in Nehemiah's inner circle?

Numerous historical records indicate there was a relationship between a king's guard and the king's cupbearer. Both were responsible for the safety and welfare of the king and his family.

Nehemiah and Hananiah most likely served King Artaxerxes together back in Susa, before the rebuilding of the wall began. It's more than feasible that Hanani and Hananiah were two of the men Nehemiah took with him when he made his midnight inspection of the city walls we read about in **Nehemiah 2:11-16**.

Nehemiah chose replacements that have many of the same characteristics as himself; God-fearing, trustworthy, loyal, kindred hearts and minds, and in total agreement with God's Big Idea for the city and people of Jerusalem.

They are unified in their hearts and minds on the end goal – helping God's people return in obedience to God.

The team you build as a leader may not have your exact personality or your same skills…or your incredible, enduring good looks! In fact, diversity of skills and talents is needed for a healthy, productive team.

But, make sure everyone on your leadership and management team is bought-in and sold-out to the Big Idea – lock, stock and barrel. You need commitment, passion and all-out effort here.

In addition to hand picking his new leadership, Nehemiah sets out a plan for keeping the Big Idea on track.

First and foremost was the continued safety of the people in Jerusalem.

> **I said to them, "The gates of Jerusalem are not to be opened until the sun is hot. While the gatekeepers are still on duty, have them shut the doors and bar them. Also appoint residents of Jerusalem as guards, some at their posts and some near their own houses." (v.3)**

Throughout the building of the wall, the builders were fearful of outsiders attacking. Nehemiah makes sure the people now beginning to re-inhabit Jerusalem feel safe and defended.

Nehemiah sets *business hours* for the city. The gates will close at night and open again after daylight.

He also returned to another strategy he used back in Nehemiah, Chapter 3...

Let the people be responsible for areas (or, in this case, gates) that are in *close* proximity to them **(v.3)**. There is ownership in maintaining your home and neighborhood. Just as people built the wall close to their home, Nehemiah was now urging these same people to serve as guards and lookouts for the entire city.

Nehemiah is so wise in this tactic. I know in my leadership life, I have several instances in which a big event was a huge success, and immediately afterward, something *negative* happened.

My daughter, Sara, is a dancer. When she was a young teenager, maybe twelve years old or so, a small group of her friends were all part of the same ballet company. She was well-trained by a former professional dancer who set high expectations and demanded precise, artistic performances from her.

It was hard work. Behind that effortless looking performance on stage was dozens of hours of technique, practice, rehearsal and training. Sara loved it. And she excelled at it.

Four of the families involved in the ballet company also attended the same church together. The girls, all Sara's age and younger, crafted their own dance to be part of the Sunday morning worship services at church.

They were taking leadership for not only the choreography of the dance, but also breaking new ground for our church in using the creativity of dance in worship.

After all, we were a Baptist church. Remember the old song by Genesis, "I Can't Dance"?

From our point of view, Phil Collins, Genesis' front-man, might as well as been Baptist *'cuz we don't dance!*

The girls were taking a risk by designing their own dance. The church was taking a risk by allowing something different to happen on a Sunday morning.

The acceptance and reception of this one dance would probably determine if our church ever used dance – or other performing arts again.

Ever.

Young leaders. Big Idea. Big Risk.

The dance performance that Sunday was flawless. The girls worked diligently, rehearsed faithfully, and practiced repetitively and *nailed* it. Our church had never experienced something like that before!

In the afterglow of a job well done, as the adrenaline and emotional rush let down an adversary reared up out of nowhere.

Someone's feelings got hurt.

A girl from another family was crying in the church lobby because she wasn't asked to be a part of the worship dance. She wasn't really a close friend of our families and our girls. She hadn't been dancing as long (or as well) as the girls who designed and performed the worship dance.

Because her daughter was emotionally shattered, the girl's mom was angry. That's what momma bears do when their kids are hurt. They fight for them.

Understandable.

They did attend the same church and did also take lessons at the same dance academy. It was a small town – that sort of overlap happens all the time.

The young girl felt that because she knew our girls, and because she went to the same dance class, that she should have been invited to dance at church. But, in fairness to Sara and her friends, there was no deliberate collusion at work.

None of the girls had maliciously intended to hurt anyone's feelings. Sara and her friends had been dancing and playing together for years. They had sleepovers all the time together. They were BFFs.

The other girl just wasn't a part of their circle.

If you have ever been in a middle school hallway listening to six girls all breathlessly expressing their daily drama and using the word, *like* a gazillion times, you would know this stuff happens all the time.

Not everyone gets invited to every party, activity or event.

And feelings get bruised.

So, in my (somewhat) objective mind, there was no reason for this girl to be hurt. To me, it was completely irrational and certainly no reason for the mom to be mad.

But, they were.

They accused the girls, and our families of leaving them out *intentionally*. They felt snubbed – and our girls were the snubbers. The situation was sort of resolved, but it was a tough life lesson for 12-year-old Sara and her friends.

In life, and especially in the life of a leader, big events with big emotions can result in big letdowns and opposition afterward. Nothing has changed in 4000 years.

Nehemiah knew this and wanted the city to be prepared and on guard for any unforeseen letdown.

Celebrate, and don't let down your guard.

Congratulate, and be watchful.

Commemorate, and do not lose sight of the Big Idea.

During the early stages of World War II, Great Britain launched the Local Defense Volunteers (LDV). This group of dedicated men, from ages 17-65 years old, were asked to help be lookouts on the English Channel coast.

They trained in combat in case Nazi Germany ever did invade Great Britain.

The nickname *Home Guard* eventually stuck.

The British War Office hoped that 150,000 volunteers would join the Home Guard. In a matter of months, 1.5 million people were part of this purely volunteer force. Ten times the number they had expected!

When a 1940 nationwide radio broadcast asked people to consider joining the Home Guard, the people of England stepped up. Just like the people of Jerusalem responded to Nehemiah's challenge in Chapter 2.

The people whom Nehemiah is suggesting stand guard in Jerusalem is the city's version of the Home Guard.

Nehemiah knew there may be an emotional letdown following the rebuilt wall. He was setting up his successors to prevent it.

I have an important question for you following your big event.

Who is the Home Guard for your organization or ministry?

Keep your people feeling safe, cared for and protected – and they will stay with you and your Big Idea. Build your wall and then do the necessary follow-up to ensure that it remains strong in the afterglow.

CHAPTER 10
A BRIEF PAUSE...
Nehemiah 7:1-3

I want to take a short pause in our story of Nehemiah and the rebuilding of the wall of Jerusalem.

If you're paying attention, you'll realize that this chapter is covering the same verses as the previous chapter. Some of my friends might call me repetitive and slow. However, I want to take a look at these verses from a different angle.

> **After the wall had been rebuilt and I had set the doors in place, the gatekeepers, the musicians and the Levites were appointed. I put in charge of Jerusalem my brother Hanani, along with Hananiah the commander of the citadel, because he was a man of integrity and feared God more than most people do. I said to them, "The gates of Jerusalem are not to be opened until the sun is hot. While the gatekeepers are still on duty, have them shut the doors and bar them. Also appoint residents of Jerusalem as guards, some at their posts and some near their own houses."**
> **(Nehemiah 7:1-3)**

We discussed in the previous chapter that Nehemiah hand-picked men to lead the next chapter in the rebuilding and repopulating of the city. He chose men who were faithful and agreed with Nehemiah's Big Idea.

Men whom Nehemiah could trust.

I want to talk about the succession of leadership in organizations or ministries. Someday you will need to step away from your current leadership role and allow someone else to take charge.

Bank on it.

Sometimes it will be of your choosing and time frame. Other times, the leadership of your ministry is looking for change and do it for you. It doesn't matter if you're a senior pastor, executive director, president or board chair of your organization – at some point, you will not be the leader. Follow-the-Leader is a fun kid's game. But, it can be very serious when someone has to follow your organization's leader and step into his/her shoes.

Apple found it serious and difficult to replace Steven Jobs (on two different occasions.)

Much of the general population of the United States wanted George Washington to be president (or king) forever. At the time, it was a major dilemma – who could ever replace George?

Has anyone really replaced Dick Clark on New Year's Rockin' Eve?

Not possible.

Here are a few situations I know of personally in which organizations did a poor job of making the switch from one leader to another:

-   An executive director, nearing retirement, spent more time and energy on a pet project that was to be her legacy, at the expense of the primary operations of the organization.

-   A board promoted a new hire into an executive role with no help or support to make the vital transition from her former government bureaucracy role to executive director, proving disastrous for her and the organization during the changeover.

-   An aggressive marketing organization hired as CEO a retired school superintendent who knew all about schools (the primary market), but knew nothing of generating earned income through sales and marketing.

Making the transition from one leader to another can cause havoc in organizations. But it does not need to be dramatic and traumatic. If done thoughtfully and well, the process can be seamless – benefiting both sides of the equation.

Replacing any leader is fraught with unknown snags and unforeseen difficulties, but through transparent communication, teamwork and finding the right person for the new position, it can be a very successful process. This is especially true if managers and leaders work hard to replace themselves.

Leslie, a dear co-worker and fellow middle manager, once said, "As a manager, I think my job is to *manage my way out of my job.*"

She felt compelled to delegate, educate, train, and coach those reporting to her in order for them to be prepared to take over when she left the organization.

It worked!

When she moved on to another professional opportunity, her department ran smoothly and flawlessly.

We personally missed her of course, but operationally, Leslie's position never skipped a beat! She replicated herself so she could be replaced.

Nehemiah ensured the same seamless, no-muss, no-fuss transition as he returned to Susa to work for the king again. He successfully prepared his followers to move forward when he stepped down.

That's leadership.

Interestingly, he did not choose people based on skill, expertise or their educational degree. Nehemiah selected men who knew the Big Idea and whom he could trust.

Hananiah was a military officer, not a city planner. Hanani was a faithful, passionate and loyal brother. We have no idea what his occupation or expertise was, but we have no reason to think he was an urban development consultant.

We know he picked men who were *committed* to the Big Idea. He picked people he *trusted*. He picked men based on their *character*.

In a time of organizational transition and change, the Big Idea needs to take precedence over any personality or individual. It needs to be *the* focus.

Many times, as a leader moves on (for whatever reason), there is a tendency to compare the incoming leader's skills and talents with the woman or man they are replacing.

That is a trait of human nature that is patently unfair to both leaders. Don't measure them side by side; instead appreciate the strengths and leadership they bring to the position.

Joe Montana was an NFL Hall of Fame quarterback. The athlete who replaced him, Steve Young, was also a Hall of Fame quarterback. They could never be mistaken for each other in style, physical presence or individual talents.

But, they excelled on the field and in leading their team. They were both champions.

The young, passionate, visionary leader who is moving onto their next newest, coolest idea may not sit well with a status quo group of corporate leaders who may feel she needs to be replaced.

The board of directors, or trustees (or whatever your flavor of governance team), is having these conversations:

"We need more systems in place. Wally Worldchanger is super passionate, but too scatterbrained to sit down long enough to talk about the growth of our organization."

"Susie Socialchange is a magnificent speaker and can really get people excited about our mission. But, she simply doesn't have the business experience to build an effective organization."

"Hipster Hannah has wonderful ideas, but her youthfulness and wardrobe aren't going to attract the kind of donors we want to build our endowment."

"Nehemiah was a good guy to start this project, even though he wasn't an architect. We need a city planner now to help organize how people come back to populate Jerusalem."

Everyone is a critic, and everyone is an expert.

Let the leader lead…and produce.

The very nature and duty of your board, elders or trustees is to help steer the course and direction of the organization. Their mindset is to build long-term capacity for long-term impact.

The very nature of a Big Idea usually is 180 degrees opposite of a formal structure, and bureaucracy. The passion and enthusiasm of the Big Idea becomes a head-on collision with the systems and structure of a well-run organization.

Andy Stanley and his leadership team at North Point Church network in the Atlanta area call this, *"A tension to manage, not a problem to solve."*

Write that on the top of your next board meeting agenda.

In any leadership transition, be certain that decisions being made are made through the filter of the Big Idea lens first.

Accounting, computer systems, webpage design, marketing, and fund-raising are all skills that can be hired, contracted, purchased or out-sourced.

The Big Idea cannot be out-sourced to a third party.

When the leader changes, don't allow your board or other stakeholders to think the Big Idea is changing, or needs to change. Don't allow the temptations of systems, professionalism and organizational charts to taint, distort or dilute the Big Idea.

It's the *Big Idea*, not the Bureaucratic Idea.

This chapter is a reminder why you, as the leader, need to keep your followers centered on God's priorities, even as you are stepping out of the leadership role and a new leader transitions into the ministry.

If you don't believe me, check out these words from someone who moved on and kept his executives and followers focused on the prize.

Then the eleven disciples went to Galilee, to the mountain where Jesus had told them to go. When they saw him, they worshiped him; but some doubted. Then Jesus came to them and said, "All authority in heaven and on earth has been given to me. Therefore go and make disciples of all nations, baptizing them in the name of the Father and of the Son and of the Holy Spirit, and teaching them to obey everything I have commanded you. And surely I am with you always, to the very end of the age." (Matthew 28:16-20)

There was no bigger Idea or more important transition than that one.

CHAPTER 11
IF YOU REBUILD IT, WILL THEY COME?
Nehemiah 7:4-8:18

Remember the movie *Fields of Dreams* with Kevin Costner and James Earl Jones? There's an epic line that spawned a thousand social media memes, *If you build it, they will come.*

That singular promise links back to our story here.

With the wall rebuilt and the city secure, Nehemiah and his other leaders now had to get people to come live in the city of Jerusalem. After all, it's clear that the city was too ruined to have many people moving back.

The city was in ruins. There was rubble everywhere with burned posts that used to be elegant gates with powerful beams. There was the eyesore of debris fields strewn across the city. The wall itself was impossible to get close to in parts due to piles and piles of stone and rock left by the builders, trying to clear out room for the new wall sections.

And, the original residents hadn't been around for 160 years. The once glorious city of God was an unrecognizable neighborhood to live in after the Babylonians had destroyed the city and taken over.

Many of the original inhabitants and their families had been scattered across the empire. Generations had passed since former residents had lived in Jerusalem.

How would anyone know if their family had even lived in Jerusalem?

To paraphrase the movie line, *If you rebuild it, will they come?*

There was also concern that since the wall had been rebuilt, people might try and take advantage of the situation. There was a fear that people would falsely claim to be from a family that had lived in Jerusalem, but did not really deserve to be allotted land in the now rebuilt area.

Greed has no limits.

Surprise, surprise.

Please do not be offended by my cynicism. People have been using lack of clarity to gain on their position, stature or wealth for thousands of years.

Why would this situation in Jerusalem being any different?

Since Nehemiah was a step ahead of evil, as always, he made certain this would be far different than past civic scandals.

> **Now the city was large and spacious, but there were few people in it, and the houses had not yet been rebuilt. So my God put it into my heart to assemble the nobles, the officials and the common people for registration by families. I found the genealogical record of those who had been the first to return. This is what I found written there. (Nehemiah 7:4-5)**

Nehemiah would make sure the families of the original residents would get their land back.

He had a record of most of the families from Jerusalem that had been scattered. **Nehemiah 7:6-73,** gives a lengthy list of the legitimate families and people who would repopulate the city.

This list is almost identical to the list found in **Ezra 2**. Ezra had begun registering eligible former citizens 12 years earlier, a documentation of great value to Nehemiah.

Many years earlier, Ezra had started the rebuilding of the Temple in Jerusalem. He had hoped it would lead to the reunification of the people. The Temple did get rebuilt, but the people did not come back together.

One primary reason was that the city was still in shambles. Even if someone's heart was wanting to obey God and His Law, they could not live in the city, near the Temple and the priests.

There was nowhere safe to stay.

If you were unfortunate enough to get caught in a Midwestern tornado, or West Coast earthquake, which destroyed a large part of your home, you wouldn't move back into your residence until it was rebuilt, right?

This was the challenge that had doomed Ezra's efforts, but Nehemiah learned from it and successfully overcame it.

The wall was rebuilt and people came from near and far; a happy ending to this movie. People could start living again in the city of their forefathers.

The territory around Jerusalem would also be populated using the list and these families. The list of names is found in the Old Testament accounts.

Nehemiah and Ezra knew the importance of remembering history. It is worth a few minutes for us to honor them by checking it out.

The people who lived in Jerusalem before the Babylonians (and others) conquered them were the lifeblood of Jewish life and culture before being occupied.

While these families were the heart of Jewish life, they may also have been the families that disobeyed God, and caused the invasion and oppression in the first place.

Think on that a moment. These might be the very families that turned their backs on God, resulting in God removing his protection over the nation of Israel. If so, they didn't deserve to be reunited with their land.

To summarize, 160 years later after these civic traitors abandon their homeland, the city walls are rebuilt and Nehemiah and Ezra are working hard to make the city great again.

And, what do they do first?

They invite back the families who caused the scattering in the first place.

What?!

That's like the Chamber of Commerce honoring a citizen with a key to the city after he had embezzled the Commerce treasury!

Yeah, let's invite the fox back into the hen house.

What in the world are Nehemiah and Ezra thinking?

Call it forgiveness. Call it a second chance.

Call it God's grace.

> **But God, being rich in mercy, because of His great
> love with which He loved us, even when we were dead
> in our transgressions, made us alive together with
> Christ (by grace you have been saved), and raised us
> up with Him, and seated us with Him in the heavenly
> places in Christ Jesus, so that in the ages to come He
> might show the surpassing riches of His grace in
> kindness toward us in Christ Jesus. For by grace you
> have been saved through faith; and that not of
> yourselves, it is the gift of God; not as a result of
> works, so that no one may boast. (Ephesians 2:4-9)**

When I was six years old, I was with some friends after church one Sunday. We were impatiently waiting for our parents to finish talking with their grown-up friends after the last hymn. We were kids. We were tired. We were bored. We wanted to go to the local buffet and well, eat all we could.

So, we decided to press our case by throwing rocks at signs in the church parking lot. I was the youngest boy in the group and eager to show the bigger kids I could throw rocks with the best of them. I hit the sign a few times, but not as often as the older boys.

I had to prove my athletic manhood so I picked up a whole handful of rocks, did my best pro baseball wind-up, and let 'em fly.

And fly they did!

Two or three of the stones caught the sign and made a machine gun rat-a-tat-tat sound as they clipped the metal sign.

Several other launched rocks found an unintended target, including the back window of a family friend's sedan!

I watched in horror as the spider web cracks exploded along the entire face of the rear windshield.

My legs morphed into tree trunks. I couldn't move. Four of my friends ran back into the church. I think in part to escape the scene of the crime, but I'm sure also to tell everyone that Greg shattered a windshield.

Immediately, I started bawling like a six-year-old. (I was six, after all.) I knew corporal punishment was headed my way. I would never live to see my first day of elementary school. I would be grounded for life. I was scared. I knew the woman that owned the car; she was a dear friend of my parents. I also knew my dad and mom would be mad. Very mad.

It's funny how memory works. I can see the parking lot, car, and the shattered rear window as if it was yesterday, but I cannot see the woman's face or remember her name.

But I recall what happened when she came out from the church and saw *her* car, and then me.

She embraced me, gave me a sloppy kiss on the cheek and said, *It's alright, Greg. Accidents happen. I forgive you.*

Even in the angst of my personal disaster, she was kind-hearted. She was gracious. She gave me a second chance.

As soon as she got the window repaired, she drove me for ice cream. I should have gotten the electric chair, not ice cream!

Nehemiah and Ezra were all about giving the former families of Jerusalem a second chance.

After decades of being in captivity and not following God's Law, both leaders knew anyone still living in the area, and those who were yet to return, would need a serious crash course in God's Word.

So, they did just that.

> **All the people came together as one in the square adjoining the Water Gate. They told Ezra the teacher of the Law to bring out the Book of the Law of Moses, which the Lord had commanded for Israel.**

> **So on the first day of the seventh month Ezra the priest brought the Law before the assembly, which was made up of men and women and all who were able to understand.**

He read it aloud from daybreak till noon as he faced the square before the Water Gate in the presence of the men, women and others who could understand.

And, all the people listened attentively to the Book of the Law.

Ezra the teacher of the Law stood on a high wooden platform built for the occasion.

Beside him on his right stood Mattithiah, Shema, Anaiah, Uriah, Hilkiah and Maaseiah; and on his left were Pedaiah, Mishael, Malkijah, Hashum, Hashbaddanah, Zechariah and Meshullam.

Ezra opened the book. All the people could see him because he was standing above them; and as he opened it, the people all stood up.

Ezra praised the Lord, the great God; and all the people lifted their hands and responded, "Amen! Amen!" Then they bowed down and worshiped the Lord with their faces to the ground.

The Levites—Jeshua, Bani, Sherebiah, Jamin, Akkub, Shabbethai, Hodiah, Maaseiah, Kelita, Azariah, Jozabad, Hanan and Pedaiah—instructed the people in the Law while the people were standing there. They read from the Book of the Law of God, making it clear and giving the meaning so that the people understood what was being read.

Then Nehemiah the governor, Ezra the priest and teacher of the Law, and the Levites who were instructing the people said to them all, "This day is holy to the Lord your God. Do not mourn or weep." For all the people had been weeping as they listened to the words of the Law.

Nehemiah said, "Go and enjoy choice food and sweet drinks, and send some to those who have nothing prepared. This day is holy to our Lord. Do not grieve, for the joy of the Lord is your strength."
(Nehemiah 8:1-10)

Even as the wall was being finished, Nehemiah had a work crew constructing this large scaffold to use as a stage in the first step in rebuilding the people.

He anticipated that the people of Jerusalem and surrounding areas needed a huge dose of God's Law. It had mostly been absent from their lives for dozens of years.

Call it a Jewish worship service.

It was, in fact, a *revival.*

Because it had been so long, not only did Ezra read the Law from *daybeak 'til noon,* there were also Levites in the crowd to explain what the Law meant and help everyone understand exactly what Ezra was reading about.

It went from sunrise until the following morning. Of course, in today's world of instant gratification and minuscule attention spans most of us back then would have gotten anxious and dozed off within minutes!

We have the intellectual staying power of a mosquito. We simply cannot keep focused that long.

Hence...REVIVAL!

The people in Jerusalem were so eager to hear God's Law that they stood around for several hours in the burning sun to hear the Law of Moses read for the first time in decades.

Nehemiah and Ezra did give the families a second chance, just like my family friend.

But they also made sure the people knew the Law, and how important it was to learn and live by it. They were not going to take the chance of the people falling back into old habits after the effort invested in rebuilding the wall.

As a leader, you *will* be in a position to give second chances. I imagine there are several people you can think of in your life that have given *you* a second chance. I've had plenty and am grateful for each extra opportunity.

Your Big Idea may even dictate that people are given another chance.

You will give second chances because people offered them to you when you needed them in the past.

You will grant second chances because you want to extend grace and encouragement to others.

Here is a true story about second chances and leadership. There was a young man who played football at the University of Louisville. He had dreams of leading his NFL team to a championship.

Instead, he found himself playing quarterback in obscurity in Pittsburgh for a semi-pro team, the Bloomfield Rams, on a rock-filled field that hurt every time he was tackled on it.

He was making $6 an hour when a teammate asked him to join him on a tryout for an NFL team. They drove to Baltimore and the Colts took a chance on the kid. (Yes, the Colts were once in Baltimore.)

The young man not only made their roster, he went on to lead them to three NFL Championships, including a Super Bowl!

Today, he is revered as one of the greatest quarterbacks in NFL history.

His name was Johnny Unitas – one of the greatest and most successful quarterbacks by any standard. Had his teammate not asked him to drive to Baltimore that day, we would never have heard of him.

The power of the second chance.

Remember Jesus Christ, who offers **all** of us a second chance. Even if you are not a churchgoer, or didn't grow up in a religious family, Jesus offers all of us a grace that we do not deserve.

He's an historical figure, not a fairy tale. He's still living and active today. He's the only faith leader who stepped out of a grave after being buried.

The Resurrection was the ultimate second chance!

Jesus will give you a second chance. If you haven't, I urge you to take Him up on it.

Because ice cream is so much more rewarding than guilt, shame and rock-throwing.

I know.

CHAPTER 12
PARTY!
Nehemiah 8:8-10:39

In the previous chapter, we looked at how Nehemiah and Ezra were giving second chances to the people of Jerusalem. A big part of that second chance involved making sure people knew, understood and applied the Word of God as they began repopulating the city.

Not only did they read and teach the Law, they also celebrated the revival and the newly re-established faith community in and around Jerusalem. There was more than a physical Wall being rebuilt.

Spiritually, the citizens were being rekindled in their hearts and souls by Almighty God.

Part of the original laws and principles God gave for His People involved the celebration of certain feasts and events that would remind people of how much He loved them, provided and protected them.

Chapters 8-10 in the Book of Nehemiah covers a fairly short period of time, roughly a month. It tells the story of how Nehemiah and Ezra used the new-found understanding of God's Law to further build the people of God, not just the walls of the city.

These verses break down into four sections. I highly recommend you read and absorb them for your own understanding as a leader.

I believe these four elements are **Convene, Celebrate, Confess** and **Covenant.**

Convene--Nehemiah 8:2

In Nehemiah's story, the Wall was rebuilt in early fall. The month Tishri, is designated as the seventh month of the Hebrew calendar **(Neh. 8:2)**. This corresponds with September-October of our current-day calendar.

It was a time of harvest, and God built in natural celebrations and commemorations for the people of Israel to remember Him and His provision during harvest.

For background, here is a brief overview of the feasts and celebrations that were a part of the ancient Jewish tradition during that time. It will give a context for how we can look at events and celebrations as leaders today.

Ezra, the priest, guided the people of Jerusalem through the celebration outlined by God's Law. Just like the reading of God's Word in the previous chapter – these rituals and celebrations had not been observed in decades.

Many of your Jewish friends still observe these today in modern times.

The first feast of the fall was the *Feast of the Trumpets*. You can read about the initial account of this in the Book of **Numbers 29:1**. It was a day for blowing trumpets (or a ram's horn) to call field workers to stop their harvesting and return to the Temple.

That must have been an inspiring sight to see.

It was, and still is, held on the first day of the seventh month. In fact, now it also symbolizes the beginning of the Jewish New Year, *Rosh Hashanah.*

In Ezra and Nehemiah's day, it was a signal for people to stop working, leave their fields and prepare for remembering God. It was a time for *convening* the people of God to come together and prepare for both a somber and celebratory time.

After spending more than a month immersed in the physical labor of wall building, I'm sure many people didn't need a second invite to stop working.

But, working your fields, you would naturally harvest everything you could, to provide for your family and to trade with neighbors.

Interestingly, God's Law even encouraged *not* harvesting everything. It is important to note that many of His rituals and traditions, including the holy sacraments, were about the *process*, not just the event.

God loves to refine our character as we approach the event or rite.

> **When you reap the harvest of your land, do not reap
> to the very edges of your field or gather the gleanings
> of your harvest. Leave them for the poor and for the
> foreigner residing among you. I am the LORD your
> God. (Leviticus 23:22)**

It is an educated guess that the Feasts of Trumpets, this *convening*, was also to ensure that people left some grain in the field. This would help the poor; *and* also serve as a reminder that God is ultimately our Provision, not only our hard work and effort.

Celebrate--Nehemiah 8:8-13

Celebrations are a huge part of our lives, aren't they?

My birthday is in late December, so sometimes it's easy for my family to get caught up in Christmas events and activities, and celebrating my birthday is an afterthought. It has never bothered me, because it's all I've ever known.

But, when I was 11, my parents went out of their way to plan a birthday party for me in the *summer*, to highlight my new year on earth.

I had a sleepover with seven to eight of my friends, who just because of the craziness of Christmas and family activities would never be able to attend my overnight party in late December.

To make it realistic, all my presents were winter-related, including hockey stick and skates, and a table-top hockey game with my favorite team as one of the competitors.

We drank hot chocolate and sipped soup, just as if we were celebrating in the dead of winter.

I had a blast, and truth be told, I probably got double birthday presents that year in June and again in December.

Bam!

It was a celebration that I fondly remembered for years. There were other parties and celebrations every year, but that one was special.

I hope there have been many celebrations during your life that are pleasantly seared in your mind to this day.

Your wedding. Your parent's 50th anniversary. The 1st birthday of your first child. Your spouse's birthday. (Forgetting your wife's birthday is punishable by death!)

Organizations also have their own celebrations in their history. It might be the date of your first big donation (still framed on the wall, is it?). Or, the groundbreaking for a new building, the date of the first meeting together as a group, or the week your ministry received that first big grant.

It might be connected to a significant event. For instance, it might be tied to a natural disaster that launched someone's Big Idea for aid that was related to the tragedy.

The commemoration doesn't necessarily have to be of a good or pleasant memory. It just has to be a historic turning point in its impact.

Here in the United States, we remember dates like **December 7, 1941; November 22, 1963;** and **September 11, 2001.** All tragic days, but ones we will forever use as a touchstone in our history.

A few days after this *convening* by trumpet call, they observed the **Day of Atonement.** This is perhaps the most holy day in the Jewish calendar. It is the day when the high priest, Ezra in our story, undergoes a number of rituals to prepare himself to enter the Holy of Holies in the Temple of God, the very place where Nehemiah's enemies tried to get him to hide in cowardice.

As I read, there really is no specific mention of the Day of Atonement in the Nehemiah story.

However, I believe Ezra did follow through with all the elements and sacrifices, and went into the temple to pray for the forgiveness of sins on behalf of the Jews.

After this somber and important day, God orchestrated the Feasts of the Booths.

> **They found written in the Law, which the Lord had commanded through Moses, that the Israelites were to live in temporary shelters during the festival of the seventh month and that they should proclaim this word and spread it throughout their towns and in Jerusalem: "Go out into the hill country and bring back branches from olive and wild olive trees, and from myrtles, palms and shade trees, to make temporary shelters"--as it is written.**

> So the people went out and brought back branches
> and built themselves temporary shelters on their own
> roofs, in their courtyards, in the courts of the house of
> God and in the square by the Water Gate and the one
> by the Gate of Ephraim. The whole company that had
> returned from exile built temporary shelters and lived
> in them. From the days of Joshua son of Nun until
> that day, the Israelites had not celebrated it like this.
> And their joy was very great. (Nehemiah 8:14-17)

And, they celebrated!

> Day after day, from the first day to the last, Ezra read
> from the Book of the Law of God. They celebrated the
> festival for seven days, and on the eighth day, in
> accordance with the regulation, there was an
> assembly. (Nehemiah 8:18)

If you know much about the Old Testament and the story of God's People, you know that they spent 40 years wandering in the wilderness.

For your reference, **Leviticus 23:40–42** is the first place we see this feast or holiday observed, shortly after the People of Israel fled from their Egyptian captivity. It is also mentioned in **Deuteronomy 16:13**, and other places in the Book of Deuteronomy.

Essentially, the Jews were supposed to go and find sturdy limbs, saplings and vines, and make a tent.

Yes, a tent.

I love camping and hiking, so this would not be a problem for me. But, I have friends whose idea of roughing it is when the Marriott is late with their room service.

A cold BLT?

Horrors!

Consider this – you have just spent 52 days rebuilding a wall, so you and your family could then rebuild your own house, so you can live in God's City again, after 160 years. And now, Nehemiah and Ezra want you to build – and live in – a *tent*.

What?!

However, after observing God's miraculous work for 52 days and seeing how Nehemiah and Ezra were committed and obedient to God, even the weary builders were caught up in how God's Spirit was powerfully moving among them.

After hearing God's Law and Promises for the first time in 160 years their hearts, souls and emotions were stirred beyond anything they had ever experienced before!

Celebrate they did. **(Neh. 8:9-11)** And camp they did. **And their joy was very great. (Neh. 8:17)**

Confess-- Nehemiah 9:1-38

Moving into Chapter 9 of Nehemiah, we see that joyous celebration deepens into the element of *confession* during this month-long revival.

> **Those of Israelite descent had separated themselves from all foreigners. They stood in their places and confessed their sins and the sins of their ancestors. They stood where they were and read from the Book of the Law of the Lord their God for a quarter of the day, and spent another quarter in confession and in worshiping the Lord their God. (Nehemiah. 9:2,3)**

Chapter 9 is dominated by one long prayer of *confession*. It isn't an ooey-gooey-oh-God-bless-us kind of prayer. This was the Sovereign God they were talking to – not some Kumbaya melodrama of sweetness and light.

It is a hard-core wow-have-we-ever-blown-it-over-and-over-again prayer, a serious, authentic *confession* seared into the soul of Almighty God, the kind of prayer we need to be communicating today.

You have heard it said, ***Confession is good for the soul.*** As I understand, this is an old Scottish proverb.
But, there is a word missing.

Open *confession is good for the soul,* is how the saying was first used. It needs to be public, transparent and for the world to see!

As a leader, you will find times that you, and perhaps your entire organization, will need to get brutally honest and contrite. It might be the way you dealt with a certain donor or client. Or, it might be how you are using your resources.

This prayer of *confession* might be dealing with a pervasive attitude that has encroached into your organization, perhaps a sense of entitlement, or a sense of defeatism.

Either way, you will need to realize this need for *confession*. As leader, *you* will need to model this remorse. Don't play the *leader card* and think you are above acknowledging your faults, and the faults of your group.

Confession provides for a reset. A *do-over* if you will. It allows others to join you and establish a new (or renewed) way of working.

I am not talking about the person that always apologizes for something and then continues to keep practicing that very sin or bad behavior, only to apologize again.

A simple definition of confession is agreement. We agree that we are not leading our organization the way we should.

We agree that we have veered off course from our main mission, or neglected key clients.

We agree that we have not been good stewards of the resources we have.

We agree that we have not compensated our staff fairly.

We agree – and we are not going to simply agree. We are going to change behavior. We are going to live, behave and lead differently.

My church some years ago had a solemn assembly. We held only one service that week (instead of two). We alerted people the reason we were doing it, and how the morning church service would be different than any other service we ever held.
Yes, we had singing, and prayer time, just like other weekends.

We also had more than an hour of confessing…of agreeing.

Some of this confession included the leaders of the church publicly agreeing that we failed in certain areas. How we treated a former pastor (poorly).

How we put off financial matters until they had become a crisis.

That sort of public confession.

And, we gently challenged individuals to also confess their sins, first to anyone in the room that needed to hear it privately, and then to share publicly. At the microphone. In front of everyone.

High risk, but dozens of people used that day to set their mind, heart, and attitude right again. They agreed to live differently. They did it in public.

They agreed to be accountable to each other.

This *confession* rolls naturally into the *covenant* promise in Chapter 10. To avoid and prevent you from being the leader, or organization, that keeps behaving badly, even after *confession*, there needs to be an agreement, or *covenant*, to stop behaving badly, and act differently.

Covenant--Nehemiah 10:1-39

Nehemiah 10 details a broad number of activities and obligations that the people are now going to live by. Let's just review a few here:

> **Not to give their daughters or sons in marriage to other (non-Jewish) groups near them. (v. 30)**

> **Not to buy, trade or do commerce with neighboring people on the Sabbath or other holy days. (v. 31)**

> **Give a set portion of their resource to the operations of God's house. (v. 32)**

> **Bring the first fruits of their crops to the house of the Lord. (v.35)**

You can read the entire chapter and see how significant and all-encompassing this covenant was...the builders are now going to follow God's Law, and they all signed it publicly.

I do not believe this was done out of fear that they might be conquered again. After all, they are still under the monarchy of the king of Persia.

No, they agreed to this covenant *because* they realized their lives could be changed. As they rebuilt the wall, they knew deep in their hearts that God would continue to protect and provide for them, as they were obedient to Him and His Laws.

Convene. Celebrate. Confess. Covenant.

As a leader, you will need to replay these four principles throughout your life and organization. Each one is uniquely powerful and singularly important, but they all fit together as one in God's power pack of wisdom, holiness and joyful success.

I frequently see these four elements translated into powerful events in the world today.

I know many private schools that have an annual dinner and silent auction that serves to *convene* and *celebrate* their accomplishments.

Most crisis pregnancy organizations I know convene for a yearly banquet to recharge their stakeholders and ministry partners, and renew their *covenant* of helping the young women and men in their community.

Many churches have a volunteer appreciation day to *celebrate* and thank the individuals and families who invest their time regularly into the operations of the church.

And, there *will* be times you will need to *confess* your own miscues, and the failings of your organizations. I have participated in this type of solemn assembly before.

It is heart-wrenching and at the same time, purifying.

It is also encouraging as an organization moves from *confession* to *covenant*. These can be major turning points for you and your followers.

Just like Nehemiah.

CHAPTER 13
IT AIN'T OVER 'TIL IT'S OVER...
Nehemiah 11-13

We are reaching the end of our story. We'll spend a few moments looking at **Chapters 11 and 12**, and then finish out Nehemiah's Big Idea and **Chapter 13**. It has been a divine pleasure narrating this great servant of God.

We have seen Nehemiah tackle a huge problem and inspire others to help.

We have seen him step *way* outside his comfort zone and become a leader because of the Big Idea God placed in his heart.

We have seen him navigate political intrigue and civil unrest, always anticipating his adversaries and intervening in an incredibly effective and successful way.

What's left in this guy's story? What else could possibly happen?

Stick around, my friends. There's more intrigue and conspiracy still to come.

Organization and Order

I said earlier in the book that sometimes lists in the Bible confuse me. I don't want to over-spiritualize here. I believe there are several insights and ideas we can glean from these biblical rosters.

I won't repeat all the text here, but we need to look at **Nehemiah, Chapter 11**. It was essentially an organizational chart of all the people moving back into Jerusalem and the surrounding area.

Priests, leaders, Levites, gatekeepers, Temple servants, and others, were all listed by name, and also by where they were going to be living.

Nehemiah's logical mind and his attention to detail glistened here once again.

He knew that once the community of Jerusalem was up and running, people needed to know who was doing what. Residents needed to know where to find information, gather resources, get their questions answered, and so on.

Even more importantly, because Nehemiah was going back to the capital of the kingdom and return to his *real job* as cupbearer. It was imperative that he leave a system (and people) in place that would maintain proper order and keep God's People moving in the right direction.

Not moving, as in traveling, but in continuing to rebuild God's *people*, just as the wall had been rebuilt.

Back in **Nehemiah, Chapter 2:4-7** when Nehemiah was asking the king for permission to go to Jerusalem, he had a detailed list of materials and letters he requested from Artaxerxes.

The king agreed to *all* of them.

Nehemiah's thinking here is no different. His mind was processing, ***What logically has to happen and be in place for Jerusalem to stay on the right path? What people need to be tasked with keeping the city running?***

Most importantly, what needed to be in place to keep God's people obeying Him?

Chapter 11 perfectly accomplished that need.

It was a beautiful combination of the right people, in the right place, as they performed the right roles. Nehemiah knew what needed to be done and he did it.

Who are *your* right people?

Are they in the most effective roles?

Are they supporting the *Big Idea* and leading *with* you?"

A Big Deal to Celebrate a *Big Idea*

Let's jump to **Nehemiah 12:27-47**. The wall was rebuilt. Nehemiah and Ezra have read the Law of God to the people living in and around Jerusalem. The important festivals have been observed, according to God's Law.

God's people are in the middle of a revival. Their hearts and minds are being renewed and a new enthusiasm for obedience to God is **in motion.**

Exciting and critical times for sure.

These exciting times needed an exciting event, like an *extravaganza*. This is what we find in the middle of **Nehemiah 12**. We have different ideas of what an extravagant event might be. Some of us believe that a fancy dinner that ends with a decadent dessert (and pricey bill!) is *extravagant*.

Others define extravagant as a grand ball, complete with tuxedos, wait-staff displaying trays of sushi and finger-food delicacies, and long-stemmed champagne flutes raised to health and happiness.

In my experience, there may be nothing more extravagant than the inauguration of the President of the United States. Nearly 250 years of peaceful transition of power is reflected in a single day when a new President is sworn into the highest office in the land.

Another example of extravagance was the wedding of the royal couple in Great Britain. Prince William, the Duke of Cambridge, married Catherine Middleton on April 28, 2011. Horse-drawn carriages…social media frenzies over hat styles…hundreds of millions of viewers on all the major media outlets…fancy dress balls…more toasts than a midnight viewing of Rocky Horror Picture Show.

Nehemiah dedicated the rebuilt wall of Jerusalem, an event not only for an entire generation, but also for future generations to remember. It needed to be a landmark event, and a spectacular extravaganza. Just like a presidential inauguration or royal wedding.

Close your eyes and picture this…musicians **(Neh. 12:28, 29)**, singers **(v. 31 & 38)**, priests **(v.30)**, leaders and city dignitaries **(v. 31)** and the entire *city* participating in the celebration and dedication.

A grand procession began at one point on the wall and continued in opposite directions. Nehemiah headed one line and Ezra the other. They circled the wall with this delegation of priests, Levites, singers, musicians and the joyous citizens of Jerusalem.

I believe that the group Ezra led was actually tracing the same path Nehemiah took on his late night wall inspection after his arrival to the city.

Fitting.

> **And on that day they offered great sacrifices, rejoicing because God had given them great joy. The women and children also rejoiced. The sound of rejoicing in Jerusalem could be heard far away. (Nehemiah 12:43)**

The sound of rejoicing in Jerusalem could be heard for miles away!

The cynic in me wishes that the rejoicing and singing resonated all the way to Sanballat's home. A final, echoing chord reminding him and all of us, of God's promise and power as His people give Him praise.

Perhaps Sanballat's cupbearer was serving crow that day.

It Ain't Over 'Til It's Over...

Even if you're not a baseball fan, you have probably heard this Yogi Berra quote, or some version of it.

We are now in the ninth inning of our story and Nehemiah has pitched a great game. The other team has stepped into the batter's box and tried to get a piece of Nehemiah. But, like a great pitcher, Nehemiah stayed ahead in the count.

Mr. Berra knew that until the last pitch, of the last batter, of the last inning, the game is still in question. As we step into **Nehemiah, Chapter 13**, we find that Nehemiah's opposition is still competing down to the last out.

Based on a true story in Yogi's experience was the fifth game of the 1956 World Series, Don Larsen was one strike away from the only perfect game in Series' history. He threw a 1-2 pitch to Dale Mitchell of the Brooklyn Dodgers who swung half-heartedly and was called out!

The catcher?

None other than Yogi Berra catching that last pitch for the final out. It was OVER! He jumped on Larsen and bear hugged him almost knocking him to the ground!

On Nehemiah's field, his masterpiece of a game was also winding down. He described the scene of the final inning even while he was back in Babylon as he wrapped up business.

> Before this, Eliashib the priest had been put in charge of the storerooms of the house of our God. He was closely associated with Tobiah, and he had provided him with a large room formerly used to store the grain offerings and incense and Temple articles, and also the tithes of grain, new wine and olive oil prescribed for the Levites, musicians and gatekeepers, as well as the contributions for the priests.
>
> But while all this was going on, I was not in Jerusalem, for in the thirty-second year of Artaxerxes king of Babylon I had returned to the king. Sometime later I asked his permission and came back to Jerusalem. Here I learned about the evil thing Eliashib had done in providing Tobiah a room in the courts of the house of God. I was greatly displeased and threw all Tobiah's household goods out of the room. I gave orders to purify the rooms, and then I put back into them the equipment of the house of God, with the grain offerings and the incense.
>
> I also learned that the portions assigned to the Levites had not been given to them, and that all the Levites and musicians responsible for the service had gone back to their own fields. So I rebuked the officials and asked them, "Why is the house of God neglected?" Then I called them together and stationed them at their posts. (Nehemiah 13:4-11)

Tobiah?

How'd he get back in our story?

Berra was right...it ain't over 'til it's OVER!

Previously in **Chapter 8**, we learned that Tobiah was deeply connected to the Jerusalem Jews, probably through marriage to a family member of Eliashib, one of the priests. This connection had been quietly at play since the wall was being rebuilt.

There was no clear timeline, but at some point, it was clear that Nehemiah returned to Susa and served again as the king's cupbearer. This incident in **Chapter 13** happened roughly 12 years after the rebuilding of the wall.

It was upon Nehemiah's second coming to Jerusalem that he found out that despite the great work God was doing in and around Jerusalem, not everything was satisfactory. There was still sin and selfishness in the midst of the revival just as there is today in your world, perhaps with people you lead, or people close to your organization or *Big Idea*.

Eliashib, a priest who has been a minor player in our story, had a family connection to Tobiah, and Tobiah convinced the priest to somehow allow him the use of a sacred room in the Temple for an apartment. The room designed for storing the tools and supplies for the operations of the Temple was now a cozy apartment.

Crazy.

I'm not sure which is more mind-blowing to me...that a priest (who knew better) was convinced to allow it, or that others in the service of the Temple didn't call it out and try to prevent it

It took Nehemiah coming back 800 miles to deal with it.

Deal with it he does.

He rebuked Eliashib and demanded that Tobiah's stuff be pitched to the curb. He made sure the room was cleansed according to God's Law and the room was again used the way it was originally intended.

As I read this part of the story, I wondered if Nehemiah knew all along that Eliashib and Tobiah were up to no good. If you read back in **Nehemiah, Chapter 10**, among all the leaders and citizens who signed a covenant with God as part of their confession, Eliashib was not listed as a signer of the covenant.

I know the narrative here is not a detailed point-by-point journal of Nehemiah's story. Perhaps, in the recording and transcribing over the years, Eliashib's name was inadvertently omitted from the story. So, I don't want to launch any speculative social media threads on the details.

Perhaps Nehemiah sensed that Eliashib was not going to fulfill the office of priest as commanded by God. Maybe, Nehemiah was just plain suspicious of Tobiah, given the underhanded ways Tobiah acted in our story.

I would have been.

No matter the details and back story, Nehemiah called out bad behavior and made it right again.

He kicked out Tobiah. He restored the proper use of Temple rooms and supplies. He reestablished the observance of the Sabbath (again).

Later in the chapter, he even gave a beat-down to some men and pulled out their hair. As much as I have speculated on some points in this story, I am at a loss for words for how to give you a practical leadership application to hair-pulling in a pay-per-view pro wrestling match.

Even 12 years later, removed from the rebuilding itself, Nehemiah's passion, tenacity and determination for God's Big Idea was as solid, strong and unequivocal as ever.

I suppose some readers may look at **Nehemiah 13** and feel a sense of hopelessness. You'd hope the people of Jerusalem would stay obedient to God. Why would Nehemiah still have to return and set things right again? Even a priest, who saw God's protection and provision in the midst of adversity and the rebuilding, couldn't stick with his faith.

If a leader of faith can't keep his faith together, how am I going to? How is a plain, ordinary person like you or me going to stay on track?

I understand how you might feel that way, and I think it's the view of a pessimist.

My sense is one of passion, resolve and grit. The Big Idea that God placed in Nehemiah's heart way back in Susa was the *driving* force compelling him to succeed over 12 difficult and combative years.

The Big Idea catapulted him into a leadership role. A role he probably didn't have as a cupbearer, but one that changed the course of the people of Israel and the city of Jerusalem forever…and one that set the stage for the arrival of John the Baptist and Jesus of Nazareth 450 years later.

I encourage you to look back at the list of needs, problems and ministry opportunities listed in **Chapter 1** of this book. It's not comprehensive and there are many other needs and issues all around us.

They are a great starting point for you.

What's *your Big Idea?*

What problem or need is under your skin so deep it won't go away?

What keeps you awake at night, dreaming of a solution to a problem?

What is God's powerful vision that you feel and sense so passionately that you cannot possibly ignore it?

That is the personally planted *Big Idea* from God – to you.

You've tried to ignore it, and yet it haunts you. You've tried to look away, and your mind's eye always returns to focus on it. Once God put it there, you will have no rest until you *act* upon it.

What is it that you feel deeply about, and at first glance, you doubt your abilities and talents to accomplish it?

If your faith is lacking, your fear is paralyzing, and you keep doubting, then the Big Idea will never happen.

But, if you'll take Almighty God at His word and commit to His sovereignty in the power and grace of the Holy Spirit, you will take the first steps in *your* 800-mile journey to today's wall that needs to be rebuilt somewhere in the world, maybe in your own community.

You can faithfully accomplish the *Big Idea* God has given you…

And lead others along the way.

Let's close by paraphrasing our hero,

> **You are doing a great work and you cannot come down. Why should the work stop while you leave it and come down? (Neh. 6:3 – NASB)**

God bless.

Gregory Long
September 12, 2017

Lessons for Leaders:

Ideas and Strategies I Wish I Learned Sooner

The next few chapters highlight ideas, principles & strategies every leader needs. They don't fit nicely into the chapter-by-chapter narrative of Nehemiah's story, but serve as an undercurrent to the rebuilding of the wall and Nehemiah's life.

They are ideas I wished I'd learned earlier in my life as a leader. I pray you will find them helpful, and use them.

CHAPTER 14
SERVANT LEADERSHIP

This may be the most important lesson I ever learned as a leader. The idea of Servant Leadership is not new, but it seems to be gaining a new generation of leaders who see a more effective way to lead their teams – *by serving.*

In my first managerial job, I was responsible for three different work teams with a total of 16 employees. We were in a growing organization. My teams were responsible for securing and delivering workshops that produced a huge portion of the organization's overall revenue. Because we were growing, we needed to keep close track of events and possible future events.

The numbers were important. As the manager of this group, I was accountable for accurate and timely projections.

My bosses had faith in me to promote me into this role and I wanted to live up to their expectations and confidence.

I was the big kahuna, the top dog, boss man. I was in charge.

I had been in leadership roles before…small group studies with my church youth group…chaperone for bike trips and swim parties. I had even spoken in front of a few weekly student events. But, this was the first time I was getting paid to be a leader and manager.

This was my chance. My big opportunity.

I almost failed miserably.

The organization was in the middle of conducting annual performance reviews for all employees. I had met and given appraisals to most of the members of my teams, and was feeling great.

I was giving insightful feedback. Setting goals for future performance. Affirming their strengths and contributions. Coaching my team members. Reminding them of how important they were to our mission

I was super leader in my mind!

During an appraisal meeting with one of my team members, she stuck a sharp pin into my inflated ego balloon.

POP! Whooooooooooooooooooooooooooosh.

After I discussed her performance and reviewed the official job performance form, I leaned back and asked, *Anything else you want to discuss?*

Yes, she said. *It's about you.*

She went on at some length (felt like hours) describing how my attitude and personality had changed since my promotion. Before I became a manager, I was kind, polite and always willing to help out.

Since my promotion, she continued, I was intrusive, aloof and generally a pompous…(well, you get the idea).

I was shell-shocked. Not by the fact that an employee called me on the carpet for being a jerk. I was shocked that I was being a jerk and needed to be called out.

I was stunned. She was completely right. I HAD become a jerk. I was now the exact person and manager I never wanted to become. Selfish. Arrogant. Full of myself.

I wanted to be a leader who was compassionate, open-minded, focused on the well-being of my staff. Boy, was I WAY off.

After a couple of days of reflection, I vowed to work at being a leader people wanted to follow. A leader that people could trust. A leader who was as concerned about people as products, polices or profit.

After considering my jerk behavior, I decided to have yet another meeting with all 16 of my team members. I had just finished giving them all one-on-one performance reviews.

I met again with all of them, one-on-one, to personally apologize for being a jerk since becoming their manager.

As I write this section, I am driving toward Hot Springs, Arkansas from my home in Central Ohio. It only seems appropriate that my drive today is just over 800 miles, the same distance that Nehemiah traveled to get to Jerusalem, the city of his forefathers.

This weekend, I am facilitating a leadership event for high school students. Kiwanis International, one of the world's foremost service organizations, has an initiative called Key Leader. It is a weekend-long camp experience that helps young people conceptualize and develop crucial leadership skills.

The overall theme of the weekend is Servant Leadership.

Many of the concepts in Key Leader have been drawn from the 1970 publication entitled, *The Servant as Leader*, by Robert K. Greenleaf. After decades of working in large corporations, Greenleaf determined that the best leaders weren't necessarily the people with the corner office, largest salary, or proper title.

In his view, leadership isn't a title or position. Leadership is the attitude and action of an individual. (If you haven't read this publication yet, it is a great introduction to the principles of servant leadership.)

Kiwanis Key Leader covers five concepts that we believe are important for young people to understand and apply in their lives. These include –

Integrity
Personal Growth
Respect
Community
Excellence

I am honored and humbled to be one of only 16 North American facilitators to work with high school students in this way.

One way that Kiwanis Key Leader helps define servant leadership for high school students is through a prism of three questions that can be asked in nearly any leadership situation.

It is based directly from Robert Greenleaf's book. And, for me, it serves as a laser beam for leaders.

We call these the *Key Leader Test* and the questions are:

1)   Is what I'm doing helping others to become stronger and more independent?

2)   Do others, or does the organization become better because of what I'm doing?

3)   Do my actions help others in my community?

Any leader, of any age, can use these three questions to help check themselves on whether or not they are *serving their followers, or demanding their followers serve them.*

You have probably guessed by now that I am a follower of Jesus Christ, and as best I can, I incorporate my faith into all areas of my personal and professional life. Jesus is probably one of the first (and finest) examples of servant leadership throughout history.

One of the examples of Jesus leading his disciples through serving them, is the story in the Gospel of **John, Chapter 13** when Jesus actually washes the feet of his followers. You need to remember the context for this scene. People were not wearing their Nikes and chucks to walk along the rocky and dusty roads in ancient Jerusalem. People's feet were scarred, dusty and dirty all the time.

The symbolic act of Jesus washing the feet of his disciples spoke more loudly than any Sunday school lesson or sermon.

Jesus wanted his disciples to know that in order to be a true follower of Christ, people had to put others first. You may remember it was about this time that the disciples were getting in arguments over which disciple was the *best* follower of Jesus.

In their mind, leadership with Jesus meant the right title for the right position. Jesus was reminding them it was *their heart's attitude and action* that was most important.

I also believe Nehemiah displayed servant leadership during the rebuilding of the wall of Jerusalem. In fact he started as a wine taster, someone who was serving the king. Nehemiah literally started as a servant, and ended up as governor of Jerusalem *not because he had the right title or the right education.*

Nehemiah had a servant heart toward God and pursued God's Big Idea, leading the people of Jerusalem to rebuild the wall by serving them first.

Nehemiah was in charge of the entourage that traveled to Jerusalem. He could have commanded one of the king's guards to take the reconnaissance lap around Jerusalem to determine the extent of the damage **(Chapter 2)**. Nehemiah wanted to see firsthand what service needed to be provided in order to rebuild the walls.

Nehemiah also exhibited servant leadership in **Chapter 5** when he confronted the pawnbrokers to give back the children and property of other Jews helping to rebuild the wall. This certainly doesn't seem like a meek and mild server in the king's court, does it? There is a sure strength in leading through serving others.

Later in **Chapter 5**, Nehemiah again serves through his governor's table by allowing others to dine at his expense and through his resources, not demanding money from the king or from those who are eating with him.

Servant leadership is a *new* buzzword in many of the college courses I teach these days. In some meetings I attend, servant leadership is more a catchphrase or soundbite that people throw around to sound relevant.

However, true servant leadership is much more than a buzzword or phrase. It's making sure your attitude and actions are serving the people who follow you, not the other way around.

Are you treating people with respect and care?

Are you giving people the resources they need to do their job, whether it be a corporate task, or as a volunteer in your organization?

Are you allowing people to take on *your* jobs and tasks, so they can grow into new skills and situations?

Are you giving people educational opportunities to build their tool kit of skills and knowledge?

Are you confirming and affirming the strengths, talents, and accomplishments of your team members?

Take another look at the Kiwanis Key Leader Test above. I believe you could ask those questions about both Jesus and Nehemiah, and their answers – as shown in their lives – point clearly to both these men *living a life of servant leadership*.

I'm still driving toward Hot Springs, Arkansas. At any point along the 800 miles Nehemiah traveled to Jerusalem, he could have thrown up his hands, given up and gone back to a cushy job in the king's court. But he exhibited servant leadership by making sure the Big Idea God planted in him was completed.

What mile marker are you on in your Big Idea journey? Are you remembering to serve your followers with your attitude, actions, and appreciation?

By serving you ARE leading.

CHAPTER 15
IDEA – POWER – AUTHORITY

This section introduces you to a concept I have used dozens, perhaps hundreds of times in many leadership situations. I believe you will find it helpful as you serve in your leadership role.

Let's jump back to **Nehemiah, Chapter 2** for a moment. The king of Persia was, for all practical purposes, the most powerful person on the face of the planet. King Artaxerxes had prestige, power, riches, control, and authority.

It was his father's army that had defeated the Babylonians, who had defeated the Israelites. And, now a trusted but still common servant, was asking for a leave of absence to travel 800 miles and rebuild the walls of another capital city.

In **Nehemiah 2:4**, the king directly asks what Nehemiah wants. And Nehemiah quickly prayed. Remember, he'd already been praying for four months.

This wasn't the first time he'd taken this Big Idea before God. But this may have been the first time he had a chance to communicate his Big Idea to anyone other than himself.

I suspect this prayer before the king lasted about 1 ½ seconds. *God, Help!*

Nehemiah asks essentially for permission to take a leave of absence from his job as cupbearer to go to a city that he had probably never been to, to help rebuild the wall that he had never seen.

When was the last time you had to ask a favor of your boss? Or your board? Or your spouse? If you have a positive, healthy relationship with any of these people – you are much more likely to be able to ask (and give) favors of them.

The king has the MOST to LOSE if God's People reunited and again started following God's commands.

The possibility that King Artaxerxes would even consider Nehemiah's request is in direct proportion to the <u>relationship</u> Nehemiah had with the king.

Obviously, I also believe God's favor was on Nehemiah, but the king was still Nehemiah's boss.

This is a concept I learned from Bill Milliken, the founder of Communities in Schools (CIS). Bill's **Idea-Power-Authority Triangle** is a practical tool to determine who may be able to help you with your Big Idea. It is essentially a relationship tool.

The Idea – Power – Authority Triangle does not work unless there are personal relationships built on trust and mutual respect.

You may also understand this as the maxim of, ***it's not <u>what</u> you know, but <u>who</u> you know*** that gets the job done.

I first learned this directly from Bill Milliken, along with some colleagues, 30 years ago. A version of this made the rounds a few years ago using actor Kevin Bacon as its focus called, *Six Degrees of Separation*.

The game was completely fun, and built on the premise that every actor in Hollywood was connected to Kevin Bacon by a trail of no more than six other actors or actresses.

Actually, this idea first surfaced in 1929 by Hungarian author Frigyes Karinthy. Basically, he determined that through *friend-of-a-friend* connections, you could meet and have a relationship with anyone else in the world.

Anyone else! In the world! In 1929, no less.

Social media websites and mobile apps, including Facebook™, Twitter™, Instagram™ and LinkedIn™ all have algorithms that are based in this thinking. Through common interests and common friends, they can help build powerful networks both personally and professionally.

I use a couple of the social media tools above, and find it uncanny how people from my past (and present) have surfaced as possible connections.

At times, it's even a bit unnerving. How did that computer figure out I knew this person?! It's fun sometimes to see a former co-worker, or high school buddy, or old girlfriend pop up on social media.

This book may have never even been written if it hadn't been for this *friend-of-a-friend* networking.

I wouldn't have reconnected with Patrick Hurley, my writing coach and editor if it hadn't been for Facebook. There was a 28-year gap in our friendship, and we reconnected on Facebook. How cool is that!

As a leader, you have the privilege and opportunity of building a network of people that will help your organization, ministry or project move forward.

Six Degrees of Separation is informal and haphazard. In other words, if you happen to realize you have a friend who knows someone else, we might get together.

Bill Milliken's Idea-Power-Authority (IPA) Triangle **is super-focused and intentional**. It is a tool you can use to define and explore relationships that will benefit your organization, mission and Big Idea.

One organization I worked with used IPA on a regular basis as we looked at new programming and partnerships. At one point, we determined we were only two people away from knocking on any door in the world.

From our relationships, among our board, our staff, or our dedicated volunteers, we knew we were only two connections from anyone.
The President of the United States. The Prime Minister of India. Heads of major corporations. Not six. TWO!

I don't say this to brag. We didn't need to contact all these politicians and executives. And we certainly did not have relationships with all of them. We didn't always have a project that would have made sense to try and knock on the door of a prime minister, minister of education or foundation executive.

However, it was encouraging and eye-opening to realize we had that type of reach and scope.

Deliberate, intentional, focused. This is the kind of effort you want to bring to your team or organization. IPA is a proven way to do this.

A requirement for the **Idea – Power – Authority Triangle** is a <u>respectful, trusting</u> relationship within all three legs of the triangle. It will not work any other way.

If you work through these exercises, I believe you will find your organization has legitimate access to a much wider range of influencers and decision-makers than you realize. Go for it!

We have all been in meetings, conferences or situations in which someone is only participating to push his or her own idea, agenda, product or service. They are self–serving and myopic, not interested in anyone else's welfare but their own. Almost intuitively we see these individuals coming from a long way away.

And, if you are like me, you run away and avoid these individuals at all costs.

This is NOT how the Idea-Power-Authority Triangle works.

I-P-A Triangle Strategy

This strategy is a way for you and your leadership team to identify potential partners and how to gain introductions and access to them. Its effectiveness is directly linked to the quality of personal relationships of the people involved.

Idea – Is defined as the idea, project, event or activity that you and your governing board want to pursue. You do not have the internal resources (people, energy, expertise, etc.) to pursue this idea on your own.

Authority – Usually an individual who can *make it happen*. They either have influence, finances, resources or knowledge which your organization needs. In this model, you do not have access to the person that has the authority to help you.

Power – A key link in this strategy. This person already has (or could build) a relationship with the Authority person above. It is the person who has the ear, attention, and influence with the Authority person. Power has the ability to introduce your Big Idea to Authority. They also have an active interest and affinity to your organization. They open the door to Authority.

AUTHORITY

IDEA ⟷ POWER

(Courtesy Bill Milliken)

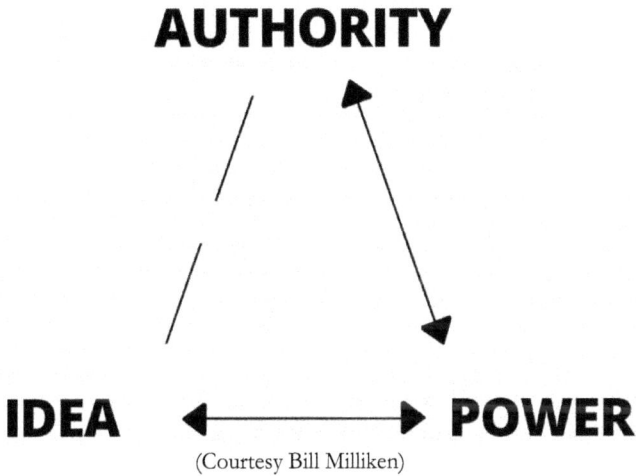

Here are a few ways you might be able to use the IPA Triangle in your organization or ministry:

- Connect with potential donors who can further your mission (Big Idea).

- Identify potential people who can help navigate political issues in state or local government. (If your organization deals with governmental or industry regulations and policies.)

- Find technology for your operations.

Who is someone, or a group, that could be an important stakeholder (Authority) that you (Idea) currently do NOT have a relationship with? Now, who do you know that knows, or has access and influence with the Authority?

Don't abuse this relationship, but do use it to help further your Big Idea.

CHAPTER 16
GROUP PHASES

I wish I had a nickel for every committee, work team or advisory group meeting I've attended. And, yes, sometimes I just attended. I didn't participate. There is a difference.

You've probably been in meetings or worked on a project with people and nothing seemed to click. For some reason, the group didn't gel and get to work effectively. There was no energy or momentum. Everything about the group seemed flat and mundane.

I've been on committees with rotating membership, and between members rolling off the team, and new people joining, I'm not even sure we ever had all the members in the same room at the same time for the same meeting, ever! The meeting membership looked more like a tag-team wrestling match.

Instead of being **H**igh **P**erformance **T**eam, it was more of a **H**ardly **P**erforming **T**eam.

I bet in your mind, you are remembering that time and group of people. Right?

Besides irregular membership and participation, another problem many groups have is just not getting anything done. Sometimes it's a difficult topic. Sometimes it's poor leadership. Sometimes it's a member (or two or three) not doing their tasks in-between meetings.

I sometimes sit in meetings and experience Déjà vu. Wait, I've been in this meeting before. We're talking about the same issues, and same possible solutions all over again. We had this conversation last meeting, or last month, or last year.

Yikes.

Your meeting has become the Ground Hog Day movie all over again. Cue Bill Murray.

How do we get off this gerbil wheel and make progress toward our Big Idea?!

One of the principles I wish I had learned earlier in my leadership journey was about groups and how they function. Or, how they may not function.

Groups do not just convene and become productive overnight or right way. Depending on the group or the topic/problem the group is trying to deal with, they may not be productive for weeks or even months.

Effective, productive groups don't just happen.

They take work. And they need leading.

One of the best and most insightful models for groups is **Forming, Storming, Norming & Performing**. This illustration of group stages was first discussed by psychologist Bruce Tuckman in an academic journal back in 1965.

Dr. Tuckman passed away in 2016, but in my experience, this model has proven itself time and time again to help me determine why my group or committee isn't getting any work done.

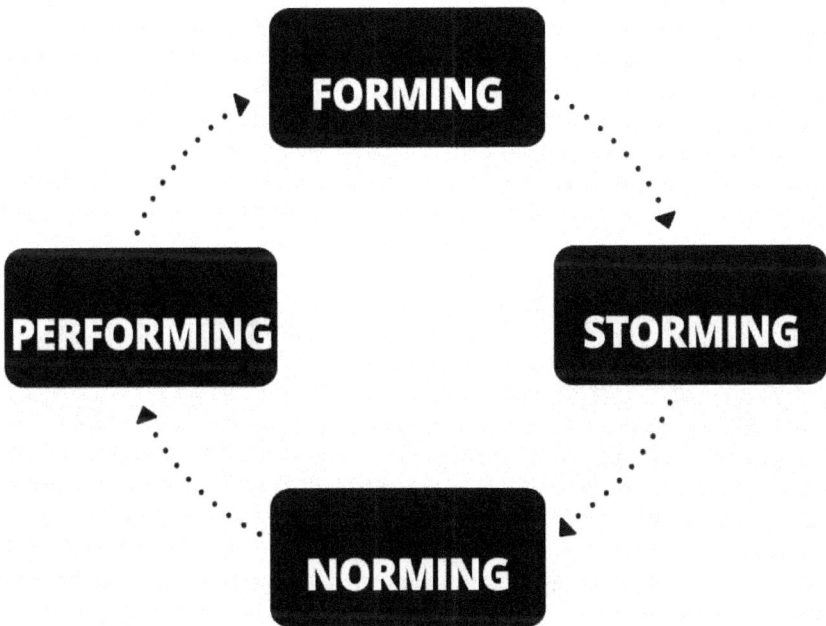

THE FOUR GROUP STAGES

Forming

The team members meet and find out the task ahead of them. It could be a problem, or the chance to pursue a great opportunity. The task needs to be connected to the Big Idea.

Once the team initially gets together, most members will tend to work independently, not including others in the work. They are enthusiastic and motivated, but may not have all the facts or resources to make any progress.

At this early stage, everyone is being polite, and are willing to nod their head at another team member's idea. However, at some point people's opinions and convictions begin to break through the politeness.

Storming

This phase may take on many shapes and flavors.

Some people in the group may simply not like the other people on the team. There is a personality clash between folks.

Someone may consistently think that their idea is way better than anyone else's, usually offending other team members and causing a conflict of the best way to tackle the task.

A sort of my-idea-is-better-than-your-idea arm wrestling contest begins.

Or, there's a perception that the work load is unequally divided, so the people who think they are investing more time and energy are frustrated and upset with the people who aren't carrying their weight.

Many times the squeaky wheel gets the attention and ends up sharing their idea, over and over and over again. As the wheel squeaks, other members are hesitant, or not able, to share their ideas for solving the problem.

Or, the group may not agree on the various tasks and priorities. No one is trying to be contentious or quarrelsome, but there is still a noticeable level of storming.

So, things get tense. This is where the going gets tough.

Now, if the group moves to the next phase, you will probably have a stronger and more effective team, because they've been able to weather the **Storming** phase.

Norming

Now, we are past our disagreements and/or egos are settled down a bit. We are figuring out how to cooperate with each other, as we lean in on the Big Idea.

We are honestly respecting, tolerating, or even celebrating the quirks and idiosyncrasies of our fellow group members. We realize we all bring something special to the committee and the Big Idea.

Group members are taking responsibility for their tasks and delivering on their assignments. People are working toward the group's goals, not their own individual wishes.

Performing

Work gets done.

People are able to work without tight supervision from the group leader. Decisions are made based on the goals and the Big Idea.

Work gets done.

There may still be disagreement on how to proceed, or on a detailed matter, but it is directed through a way that is legitimate and productive. There is no backstabbing or doing an end-run around other team members.

Work gets done.

The crazy thing I have experienced is that nearly any time the membership of the group changes – even slightly – the group has a tendency to revert back to **Forming** again, and the process starts all over.

So, even if the current meeting has a different group of people, it may be **Forming** for that particular meeting. If you have rotating members, because of office terms, etc., you may need to build the team every time it's together.

This may seem frustrating, especially to a leader who is living God's Big Idea every hour of every day.

The Four Stages in Nehemiah's Big Idea

If you think about the four stages of group development, the story of Nehemiah and his Big Idea reflect the same flow of group dynamics.

Forming (Nehemiah Style)

In the early stages of the book, shortly after Nehemiah arrives, the people living in and around the destroyed city are revitalized and energized by Nehemiah's passion. They are amped up by his vision and the way God worked in the heart of King Artaxerxes.

Like many groups just **Forming**, there is an excitement and passion around the unity of a common goal. Review **Nehemiah, Chapters 1 and 2** for a reminder.

Huzzah!

Storming (Nehemiah Style)

As the complex project of rebuilding begins, some of the early enthusiasm and unity begins to wear off. Many of the people helping rebuild the wall are becoming weary and uncertain about their ability to protect themselves from outside attack while also doing the physical labor of wall construction.

At the same time, the governors responsible for the regions outside the city of Jerusalem realize that their influence and power will be greatly diminished if the wall is rebuilt to completion and the people of Israel come back together under the law of God. They try to influence the builders by threatening, mocking and criticizing the work and the workers.

Remember in **Chapter 4**, when Sanballat and his crew show up and start to wage war against Nehemiah and the builders?

Then again in **Chapter 5**, Nehemiah needs to stand up to people within his own ranks who are forcing builders and their families to pawn their sons, daughters, and land to buy food during a time of drought and famine.

Given all this **Storming** – it's a wonder the wall was ever completed!

Norming (Nehemiah Style)

After some appropriate intervention on the part of Nehemiah, the workers again rally and continue their efforts at rebuilding the wall of Jerusalem. Despite threat of little or no food, loss of whatever minimal property they still own, and the threat of military attacks from outside – the people again focus on the common goal – and get back to work.

Performing (Nehemiah Style)

The fourth stage that most groups experience is **Performing**. In the case of the Jerusalem builders, the people (at last) continued their work. An entire wall is completed except for the doors and gates **(Neh. 6:1)**. Even then, there was a last-ditch effort to bring on another storm, through the rest of **Nehemiah, Chapter 6**.

Still, a unified people on a visionary project (Big Idea) allowed the workers to complete the work in only 52 days. If you have ever taken on a construction project within your church or organization, or even a *simple* remodeling project at home, this timeline alone may surely seem like a miracle!

Talk about high performance teams!

I believe another example of **Performing** shows up in **Nehemiah, Chapters 8 and 9**. All the people living in and near Jerusalem come together for a lengthy, and I mean lengthy, time of reading God's Law. The Priests and the Levites (the leaders) read the promises and Law of God, and helped the people understand it.

This hadn't been done in decades. In addition to the wall of Jerusalem being rebuilt, the people of Jerusalem were restored and revived.

Getting Work Done

Ok, so as a leader working toward God's Big Idea, how do you get a group to work through all four stages?

Here are a few ideas for each phase that might be helpful. This is not meant to be an all-inclusive list. Your mileage may vary, because your group and situation is unique.

Keeping on Track with Forming

I love to ask questions and build conversation around the purpose of the group every time we meet. It helps keep people focused on the Big Idea. It also helps me, as the team leader determine where we are as a group.

Typical questions I might ask when we meet:

1) How are we doing as a team? Do we agree with the progress we are (or aren't) making? If there are different views on progress, can we identify the differences?

2) What might we accomplish today (this meeting) that would move us forward toward our Big Idea? How will we know we've made progress?

Keeping on Track with Storming

1) Do we have questions since the last meeting on the purpose of the group? Are we all heading in the same direction? (These types of questions give people a chance to share their opinion, without talking over a squeaky wheel.)

2) How are you feeling about our progress? Are we moving forward as quickly as you expected? What is keeping us from being productive? How can we stop spinning our wheels and get traction?

Keeping on Track with Norming

1) How are we doing with our individual tasks? Please share about the progress you are making and what has been accomplished.

2) Are there ways other members of the group can help you?

3) What are the next steps for us as a group? Let's set mini-goals to complete before our next meeting.

Keeping on Track with Performing

This phase requires some cheerleading, so people continue their progress and see how their contributions are making a positive difference toward the Big Idea. Be sure to celebrate even small accomplishments every chance you can.

Roll up your own sleeves and keep asking team members how you can help. This displays Servant Leadership and keeps you informed on progress. You may be able to anticipate roadblocks or slowdowns before they cause problems.

We're All in This Together

Every group goes through these stages.

Sometimes the group interaction will be so blatant and obvious, you will see it clearly.

Other times, the four stages will blur together in more subtle ways. However, every group, committee and work team will go through these.

As the leader, you can help identify and manage how your group flows and progresses through these stages.

Just as Nehemiah did, you can, too.

Huzzah!

CHAPTER 17
STRATEGIC PLANNING, BIG IDEAS, AND SOLVING PROBLEMS

Most every organization has a mission statement of some type. Some are very formal with flowery wording. Others are simple, direct statements alerting the public to your organization's purpose. Unfortunately, too many times you may read the mission statement of an organization but cannot tell it apart from another organization. The mission statement is too general, too vague, too generic, too, well – bland.

In many organizations, the mission statement is not compelling or motivating. Many mission statements sound common and mundane. Here's a fictional example:

At XYZ Ministry, we are dedicated to helping our staff and volunteers help others, so they can help themselves, so they eventually help others. Oh, and we believe in World Peace.

Well, I hope it's fictional.

I appreciate Bobb Biehl's insights on organizational mission and goals. In his book, *Stop Setting Goals – If You Would Rather Solve Problems*, he states that:

15%	People are goal-oriented
80%	People are problem–oriented
5%	People are opportunity-oriented

So many mission statements are goal-focused. Unfortunately, sometimes with no compelling or motivating wording around a vague goal.

Biehl suggests that if we have a goal-oriented mission statement, we may have already lost 80% of our potential followers.

Right up front, we may be alienating 80% of our potential volunteers, donors, followers and stakeholders. However, a mission statement that clearly states how our organization is solving problems compels and draws a huge majority of people to our efforts.

What if Nehemiah had lived in the present day, with our organizational focus on mission statements and long-range strategic plans? How might his mission have read? Here are two thoughts:

The Mission of the Children of God is to follow the Law of Moses and all its sacrifices. In doing so, we will be a mighty nation, prospering in all we do and conquering the nations that do not honor the God of Israel. After we accomplish this, then God will gather us back together and rebuild the walls of our capital city, Jerusalem.

- OR -

I need to rebuild the wall!

My view is that Nehemiah was an incredibly practical individual. This is demonstrated time after time throughout Nehemiah's decisions, actions and his relationship with his followers.

No flowery, long-winded mission statement for Nehemiah. Direct. To the point. No nonsense. His focus for four months of fasting and prayer. Jerusalem is in ruins. All his energy was directed to one goal, not a five-year strategic plan.

He wasn't following a bland mission statement that could be copied and pasted by a dozen organizations. Deep in his heart, Nehemiah had a laser-focus problem to solve; he needed to Rebuild the Wall.

Hard Times

In 2009, virtually every non-profit organization (NPO) I worked with or knew about was facing difficult circumstances. At that time, the worldwide economic downturn decreased most organizations' contributions and gifts. Many families and individuals found themselves with increasing debt and/or a home not worth its mortgage. Many people were losing their jobs and livelihood.

Extraordinary measures were enacted to help prop up industries, including banking and automakers. There was, however, no stimulus plan for nonprofits (NPOs) and faith-based ministries.

Don't get me wrong, I don't think government should bail out NPOs and other charitable or benevolent groups. But ordinary citizens and taxpayers, who support many local organizations, churches and charities, were regrouping due to their own financial struggles.

Sharp declines in gifts and contributions forced NPOs and ministries to regroup as well.

Many charities didn't make it. Some closed their doors. Many reduced services and saw their impact minimized. Others merged with (hopefully) like-minded organizations.

Hard times.

The nonprofits and ministries that survived were the groups that stayed focused and energized by their mission. Their dedication to accomplishing their mission (read: solving problems) drove them and sustained them through hard times.

At the time of the Persian Empire, the Israelites were in hard times.

Nehemiah was convinced that he had to do something. Something Big. He knew enough about the Word of God that he knew God wanted something better than captivity for His people.

Nehemiah was using God's promises to drive his personal mission.

Nehemiah was all about solving problems.

Are you?

CHAPTER 18
FIND A MENTOR

If you look at professional athletes or Olympic caliber athletes, you'll see that even the best individual players in their sport have a team built around them to help them succeed and achieve their goals.

A singles tennis player, swimmer, or track and field athlete, may be the only person on the field or track at a given moment, but there are multitudes of people behind the scenes helping them do their best.

Nutritionists, dietitians, sports therapists, trainers, sparring partners, coaches and a whole host of other support team members help a single individual perform at their best.

Being an effective leader is no different.

You need to be aware of this, as well as prepared to identify and find those team members who can help you do your best. Knowing what I know now, if I were a new leader all over again, *one of the first people I would try to recruit to be part of my support team would be a mentor* (or two or three).

No matter how wise, strong, smart, or put-together you are – you want someone, a close confidant you can go to at any time. A mentor.

I've been enormously blessed to have several mentors in my life and expect to have a few more before I finish this race.

The reasons for having a close mentor seem so obvious, I almost didn't include a section on it in this book. However, humor me, and let's discuss mentors, even if it's blatantly obvious.

The big advantage to having a mentor is they are simply a source of great encouragement and support.

As a leader, many times you get stuck in situations in which you are being called on to make difficult decisions, choosing between competing ideas, or dealing with antagonists and backlash (not unlike Nehemiah).

A mentor is someone who probably has been through similar situations, and understands exactly the perceptions and emotions you're experiencing. They bring focused eyes and a clear heart to situations and circumstances that may cause your eyes to blur and your heart to lean subjectively one way or the other.

Sometimes your mentor is just great to have on hand to give you an *atta girl* or *way to go* comment when they know you have accomplished something strategic, or an important event.

At the end of a huge fundraising banquet, an important board meeting, or other significant event, many times it's your mentor who understands what you invested in energy, time and commitment, much more so than most of the other people attending that event.

Your mentor(s) have probably also gone through something similar and can relate in a very personal and deep way about what you accomplished.

I've been fortunate to have a number of mentors during my life. All of them have become dear friends whom I still stay in contact with today, even though we're not in any sort of formal mentor relationship at the moment. As you identify and build relationships with your mentors, you will (probably) have life-long friends as an extra bonus.

Dave is one of my good friends and colleagues. He really was the man who taught me how to write. I was an okay writer before we met.

Dave's background as a college and advanced-placement high school teacher of literature and grammar challenged me to be more articulate, more precise, and more concise in my writing. Most all I've neglected in this book. (Sorry, Dave.)

Now when I first met Dave as a co-worker, I was nowhere near ready to write a book. But he challenged my thinking. He challenged my sentence structure, *critiquing and encouraging* me at the same time.

Dave started out as my supervisor in a growing nonprofit organization. Our friendship has endured for nearly 30 years. We still share a cup of coffee or lunch occasionally, always laughing over situations or experiences (or personalities) that we fondly recall.

When I was ready to take on a book project (this book), Patrick showed up as a mentor. Pat was the main speaker at a conference I attended in my junior year of high school. He was funny, insightful, and spoke truth. The path and trajectory of my faith and life was forever altered after this conference. Thirty years later, Pat and I reconnected via social media.

That reconnection led to Pat mentoring me as my editor and writing coach. This book may not ever have been finished or published without Pat's guidance and help.

Dave and Clay were the men who really modeled for me how to facilitate a group or a meeting. Perhaps you've heard the old adage, *A guide on the side, not a sage on the stage.* If you look in the dictionary under the word *facilitate,* the basic definition is *to make easy.*

Your goal as leader for any sort of meeting, whether it's a board meeting with five or six people, or an orientation workshop for new volunteers, is to facilitate, to make it easy for the group to be productive and reach its goals.

Leaders talk about leading a meeting or spearheading a discussion. In fact, you're actually trying to facilitate that group, making progress together around a common agenda, theme or topic.

Over the years, I've become very adept and competent in facilitating, reading different groups of people of all sizes, backgrounds, and experiences. Most of the ability I have now to step into the room with (usually) disparate individuals and help guide them to achieving a common goal has really come from my work with Dave and Clay.

The relationship between Dave and Clay was very different, even though they both served as my mentors. Clay, for instance, was never my supervisor or my boss. We never worked together, side-by-side, in an office environment. But, I always bumped into Clay at various events where he was facilitating a group of teachers or volunteers.

I've told Clay a number of times that when I get in front of a group, I feel like I'm channeling my inner Clay in order to help the group make progress.

Again, a very different relationship than the one with Dave. Nonetheless they mentored me in facilitating groups, asking relevant questions, and throwing questions back to the group when the group needed to find their own answer, and not have me deliver cookie-cutter responses.

Another mentor that I have the utmost respect and admiration for is Mike. Mike was first a coworker and colleague, then a supervisor, and ultimately a dear friend.

Mike demonstrated to me ways to gently encourage individuals, regardless of the professional or personal situation. We worked on organizational partnerships together.

We arm-wrestled those same partners over huge mission implications, and also over the smallest details to communicate our organizational partnerships and respect our partners' needs and goals.

Mike also modeled for me how to be humble and deeply genuine when dealing with individuals. Mike was firm and encouraging. He was also honest, yet gentle when giving important feedback regarding your decisions or personal performance.

Another key element that all the above mentors helped me understand was the need for accountability and ownership. Whether personal or professional, everyone needs to be both encouraged and also held accountable for getting results.

For a new leader, or young leader, this is especially important.

Many times your mentor can help hold you accountable for elements of your professional life your board, staff, and volunteers may not need to know about. No, I'm not talking of some dark, hidden sin or blemish. (Although if that needs to be dealt with, a mentor is a great relationship to help you address a deep-seated, personal problem.)

However, you may be able to share some of your behind-the-scenes, inner anxieties, perceptions and frustrations with your mentor that you may not be ready to share with other members of your leadership team.

This doesn't mean in my view that you need to be secretive with your board or other leaders. However, I do believe *not everyone* needs to know *every single emotion, frustration, and thought every single moment.* Some of these are simply reserved for my mentor, or others close to me. The entire world doesn't need to know.

Sorry Twitter, Facebook, and other social media.

All mentor relationships look different. I know some people who have entered into a formal arrangement. For instance, they agreed to a certain number of meetings over a certain period of time. They may have agreed to a specific agenda or topic to discuss.

None of it needs to be formal or that systematized. In fact, I can't even say I've actually ever looked for a mentor. God has always brought them very naturally into my life – even *before I knew I needed* a mentor.

I meet regularly with three different men. One is a single guy just starting out with his own business.

One is a married man with young kids who is transitioning from a 40-hour office job to an entrepreneurial, self-employed business owner.

The third is a man slightly older than me, but we serve on a team together, and I have served in this role longer. He approached me to help clarify the team meetings and give a historical view on some of the actions we take.

They all happened differently, and none have an expiration date.

There's no single right way to enter into a mentor relationship. The most important fact is *you need to have one.*

Preferably, you'll identify two or three mentors who can assist you with different aspects of your personal and professional life as you move forward on this journey of leadership.

The last person that comes to mind when I think of the word mentor is Craig. God brought Craig into my path when I was a junior in high school and ready to make lots of bad decisions. In fact, I had already made plenty. Then God brought Craig into my life.

Craig mentored and discipled me in the basics of understanding God's principles. He helped me with my general understanding of how to study the Bible and apply it to my life. He demonstrated for me the importance of reaching out to others who don't know Jesus.

Craig was a huge part of my life for a couple of years, and then we both went different directions because we were in different seasons of life. Craig went on to seminary; I got married and started a career. We've stayed in touch sporadically over the years. Even so, I still have rich fond memories of discussions and prayer time with Craig.

God's timing was certainly providential and miraculous. Rather than continuing to make really poor (dare I say stupid) decisions, the relationship with Craig changed the trajectory of my life – to a direction that I will be forever grateful.

Much of this section about mentors, is really common sense, right? So much so we may overlook the importance of mentors and their role in our life and leadership.

So, go find a mentor for yourself. *Now.*

Mentors are an important element for all leaders. They come in all shapes and sizes and varieties throughout various seasons of your life.
There is no single right way to work with a mentor or potential mentor.

They will provide an outlet to help you keep from making stupid decisions.

They will help keep you accountable to your personal and professional goals.

And, they may turn into incredible friendships and sources of encouragement, support and laughter.

I often wonder who was Nehemiah's mentor?

Who did he go to when he needed a good laugh?

Now it's *your* turn to pursue the BIG Idea that God has placed on your heart. Go be a Nehemiah!

Select Resources Used

Ezra & Nehemiah: An Introduction & Commentary, by Derek Kinder
(Tyndale Old Testament Commentaries, D.J. Wiseman, General; Editor)

Nehemiah: Experiencing the Good Hand of God, by John MacArthur

Various internet-based searches & online articles & commentaries

Visioneering: God's Blueprint for Developing and Maintaining Vision, by
Andy Stanley

Zondervan Pictorial Encyclopedia of the Bible, in Five Volumes,
Merrill C. Tenney, General Editor

The NonProfit Authority

Gregory Long is CEO and Lead Developer with The NonProfit Authority. He is part of a team with more than 170 years combined experience in Development Consulting, Nonprofit Management & Leadership Training.

The NonProfit Authority has helped ministries around the world survive, adapt, and thrive in a rapidly changing world:

Nearly 40 countries, 3500 clients, close to a billion dollars raised for God's Kingdom work.

Vision isn't the issue — capacity is.

We provide the tools and expertise, so you can accomplish your God-given mission.

Online Certification, Training & Consulting

Your mission is too important to guess at what works.

Accelerate your impact.

www.npauthority.com

info@npauthority.com

1-740-258-1097

The NonProfit Authority
PO Box 110
Granville, Ohio 43023

Author Contact Information

Greg is available to help your ministry or non-profit organization.

Keynote & plenary speeches

Workshops for staff, leaders and volunteers

Retreats for leadership & board members

One-on-one consulting phone calls & meetings

Full-service Consulting and Education in Development, Leadership and Board Training, Capital Campaigns, Feasibility Audits and Professional Certification

Gregory Long, M.A.

Greg@NPAuthority.com

Gregory Long

@GregoryALong

www.NPAuthority.com

www.ingramcontent.com/pod-product-compliance
Lightning Source LLC
Chambersburg PA
CBHW070121100426
42744CB00010B/1894